# THE ILLUMINATED RUMI

BROADWAY BOOKS  NEW YORK

For
Bawa Muhaiyaddeen

*Reviver of the Light*

FIRST EDITION

Designed by Michael Green. My deep appreciation to the many, mostly anonymous visionary artists of diverse traditions whose work inspires and informs this book. It was fashioned within a new tradition now being shaped which is linked to our own High Middle Ages. At that time, it is said, artists were not so much creative personalities trying to "express themselves," but conspirators in the process of discovering and refining a visual language that could convey a living sense of the sacred. If an artist in Flanders got an Adam and Eve just right, illuminators in Milan and Paris would quickly adopt it into their canon. If an image was true, it "belonged" to the Great Mystery, and it would be foolish not to utilize it. This work is presented in similar spirit to all those engaged, once again, in finding a fresh vision of the sacred.

ISBN 0-7679-0002-2 • 96 97 98 99 00 10 9 8 7 6

# Come

**Come, Come. Come, Come!**

Come, whoever you are! Wanderer, worshipper, lover of leaving

This is not a caravan of despair. It doesn't matter if you've broken your vow a thousand times, still

and yet again

Come!

# Contents

GREED

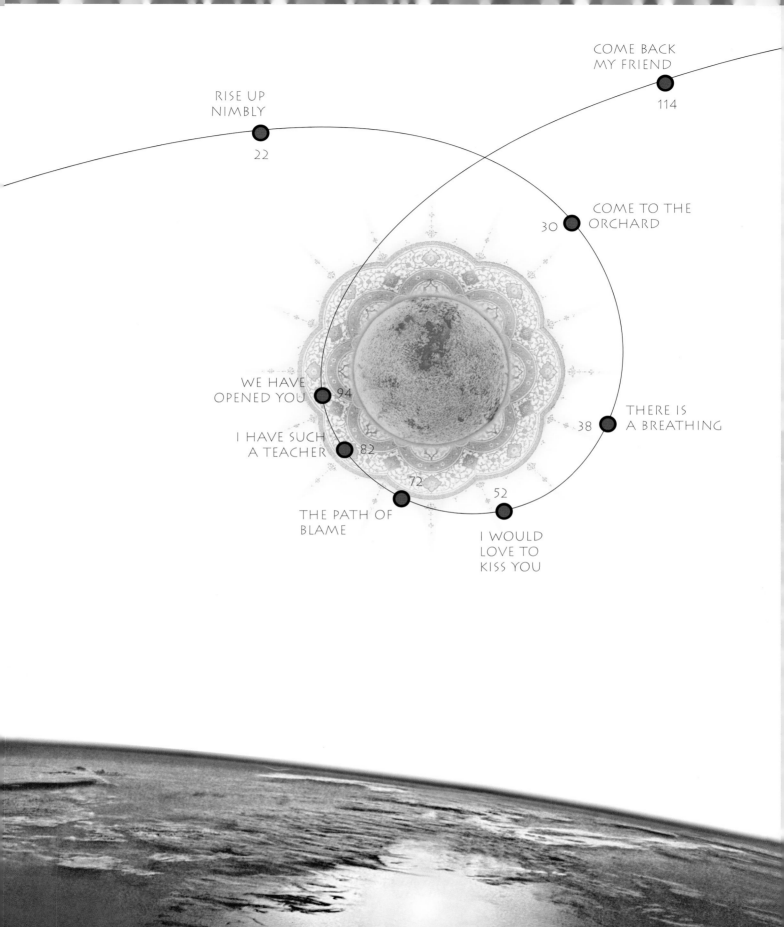

COME BACK
MY FRIEND
114

RISE UP
NIMBLY
22

COME TO THE
ORCHARD
30

WE HAVE
OPENED YOU
94

THERE IS
A BREATHING
38

I HAVE SUCH
A TEACHER
82

72

52

THE PATH OF
BLAME

I WOULD
LOVE TO
KISS YOU

# WHO ARE THESE TWO?

JELALUDDIN RUMI AND SHAMS OF TABRIZ.

The meeting of Rumi and Shams was a grand event in the mystical evolution of the planet. With their friendship, categories of teacher and student, lover and beloved, master and disciple, dissolved.

Jelaluddin Rumi was born in the remote town of Balkh, in what is now Afghanistan. He lived most of his life in Konya, Turkey, which in the 13th century was a meeting point for many cultures at the Western edge of the Silk Road, a place where Muslim, Christian, Hindu, and even Buddhist travelers mingled.

Rumi, at the age of thirty-seven, had become an accomplished doctor of theology, the center of his own divinity school. He was a venusian lover of the beautiful and the good, a scholar, and artist.

Shams was a wandering dervish monk, rough-hewn and sinewy. A street bodhisattva who mingled with laborers and camel drivers, he had no school. People spontaneously gathered around him, though he was given to slipping out side doors and leaving town when it happened. He did not want followers or fame; he only wanted to find one person vast enough in spirit to be his companion.

He met Rumi in Konya.

As Rumi was riding a donkey through the marketplace, surrounded by a knot of disciples, a stranger with piercing eyes stepped from a doorway and seized his bridle. The stranger challenged him:

"Who is greater, Muhammad or Bestami?"

Bestami was a legendary Sufi master given to ecstatic merging with God, then crying out with mystical candor that he and the Godhead were one! Muhammad was the founder of their tradition, the anointed one, but his greatness resided in his stature as *messenger* of God. So who was greater?

Rumi gave the approved answer, "Muhammad."

"But Bestami said, 'I am the Glory!' Muhammad said, ' I cannot praise you enough!'"

As Rumi was about to reply, he realized that this was no seminary debate about the mysteries. In a dusty marketplace in south central Anatolia, he had come face to face with the Mystery.

6

AND IN ONE PURE OUTRAGEOUS ACT OF FAITH, RUMI DOVE THROUGH.
IN AN INSTANT OF MYSTICAL ANNIHILATION, FIRE MET FIRE, OCEAN OCEAN,
AND RUMI FELL INTO PURE BEING.
LATER, HE WOULD SAY,
"WHAT I ONCE THOUGHT OF AS GOD I MET TODAY
AS A HUMAN BEING."

To the outside world, it is only recorded that, at Shams' question,
Rumi "tumbled from his saddle to the ground, unconscious."

When Rumi revived, lying on the ground, he answered, "Bestami took one swallow of knowledge and thought that that was all, but for Muhammad the majesty was continually unfolding."

Shams felt the depth of the answer. *This was the one he had sought.*

The two began a series of months-long retreats into solitude where they entered into a deep communion of words and silence called *sohbet.* Who can say what transpired there? We can only guess that Rumi endured the refining fires of a deep spiritual purification.

But some of Rumi's students saw their beloved teacher being spirited away by a madman, and their intrigues forced Shams to leave Konya. After a time Rumi sent his son, Sultan Veled, to bring Shams back. He found him in Damascus, playing cards in a tavern with a young man from the West, the wastrel later to become Francis of Assisi. The young man was cheating. When the entourage treated Shams like an emperor of the spirit, Francis confessed and attempted to give Shams the money back.

"No," said Shams, "take it to our friends in the West."

Shams was forced into exile several times, but he always returned at Rumi's request. Finally on December 5, 1247, fanatics in the community took Shams' life. The body disappeared. Rumi wandered for months—desolate in disbelief that his companion was really gone. One day in Damascus, he realized there was no longer a need to search. Shams was with him, in him. Rumi *embodied* the Friendship. With this final illumination, he began singing the spontaneous poetry of such beauty and perfection that it is now loved and revered across the world as revelation.

Who was Shams? The name, which actually translates as *the sun,* becomes a charged hieroglyph constantly reappearing in Rumi's poetry. Perhaps it should be shown as ☀ Shams ☀, the better to remember the radiant energy presence flaring through the mortal form. The growing field between these two, formless source and form, Rumi calls *the Friend.*

When Rumi died, he was mourned by Christians and Jews, as well as Muslims and Buddhists. While he did his spiritual spadework within the patterns of Islamic Sufism, his whole life was a witness to the boundless universality of the Heart. Accordingly, in illuminating his words, we have felt it appropriate to draw on images from all the sacred traditions, including some that Rumi himself could hardly have been aware of. His vision was whole-world work and the poetry was part of the soul-unfolding done in a learning community. Sufis are loved the world over for reminding us that the glory is our inner reality, the outer being a kind of language that explains THAT. *Love is the religion. The universe is the book.*

All of this poetry can be heard as Rumi's continuing conversation with Shams of Tabriz, an exploration of what it is to be together in God. But the stories that speak of this are at a distance from that center. The real story comes from a love-source that cannot be understood with intellect, but known only as a person is known. It is not meant to be explicated, but felt as music, as presence. These illuminations are a deliberate attempt to slow our pace down, to find a sacred space where this can happen. Listen with what Rumi called "The ear in the center of the chest." "*Hear,*" he begs us. "Hear what's behind what I say . . ."

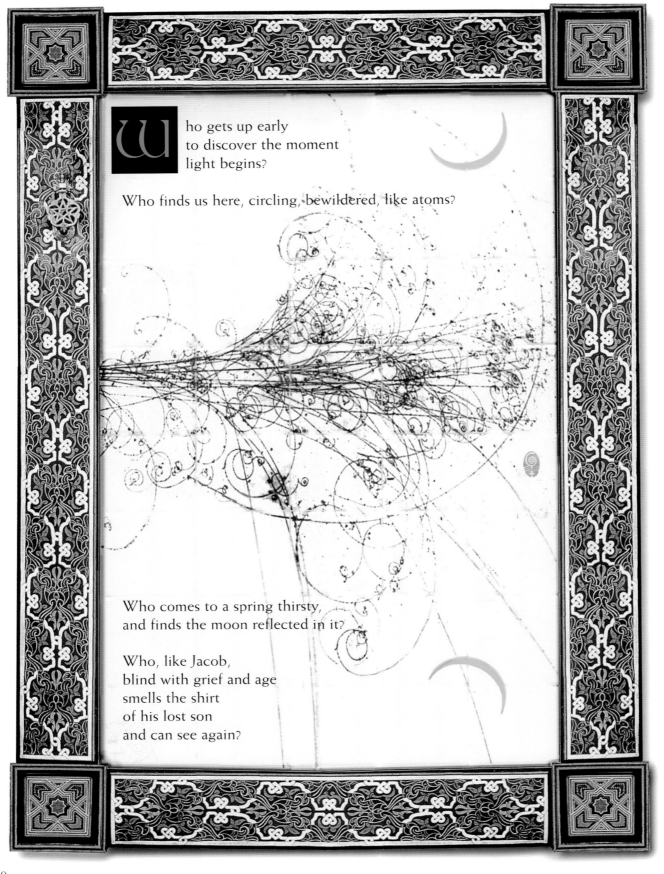

Who gets up early
to discover the moment
light begins?

Who finds us here, circling, bewildered, like atoms?

Who comes to a spring thirsty,
and finds the moon reflected in it?

Who, like Jacob,
blind with grief and age
smells the shirt
of his lost son
and can see again?

W ho lets a bucket down and brings up
a flowing prophet? Or like Moses,
goes for fire and finds
what burns inside the sunrise?

Jesus slips into a house to escape enemies,
and opens a door to the other world.
Solomon cuts open a fish,
and there's a gold ring.
Omar storms in to kill the Prophet
and leaves with blessings.
Chase a deer and end up everywhere!

An oyster opens his mouth
to swallow one drop.
Now there's a pearl.
A vagrant wanders empty ruins.
Suddenly he's wealthy.

But don't be satisfied with poems
and stories of how things
have gone with others.

Unfold your own myth,
without complicated explanation,
so everyone will understand
the passage,

W E  H A V E  O P E N E D  Y O U

Start walking toward Shams.

Your legs will get heavy
and tired. Then comes a moment
of feeling the wings you've grown,
lifting.

A life-myth begins to get interesting when a deep discontent with one's direction, or even with one's personality, arises. Sometimes this happens when you meet a living example of a whole other possibility: one of those enlightened beings, variously called saint, bodhisattva, tzadik, gnani, and many other names. In the Sufic tradition such a person is called a True Human Being.

This human shape is a ghost
made of distraction and pain.
Sometimes pure light, sometimes cruel,
trying wildly to open,
this image tightly held within itself.

uting and dream interpreting. At crucial moments the Joseph story focuses on his garment, which can be seen as the heart-covering. His brothers bring back the coat of many colors with false blood on it, saying Joseph has been killed by wolves. The legend of Zuleikha, the Egyptian woman in love with Joseph, parallels his unfolding story and continues with the shirt imagery. She clings to his shirt and tears it from his back. Finally, not in the Genesis account but from Islamic sources, Joseph gives the brothers his Egyptian shirt to lay over Jacob's blinded eyes. The fragrance of Joseph's living body restores his father's sight, and the connection with Egypt turns abundant.

## THE DREAM IN PRISON

Rumi was one of those, who slipped back into what Zorba the Greek called the whole catastrophe. He seems to rejoin the rest of us. Complacent, manic with new projects, bored, chilled by night-fears, and yet he transmuted the predicament of human existence into poetry.

Even in translation there is power in words when they source from a blessed state. It's like pressing your ear to the door of a huge power generating station: you hear someone talking . . . but underneath, you make out the hum of vast turbines.

The catastrophe and triumphs of two of the Old Testament's most compelling characters, Joseph and his father Jacob, often figure in Rumi's poetry. Joseph was sold by his brothers into slavery in Egypt, gradually came to power there, and made a complicated back-and-forth trading route between his soul-land and his Egyptian work—grain-distrib-

Egypt is transformed from *within* by the opening of the heart. The physical beauty of Joseph and his giving out of grain illuminates the way that human beings change. Zuleikha *becomes* the saint of her longing. And the darkness of the well that Joseph sits at the bottom of earlier in the story is recognized as a visionary place. From there, the glory to come can be glimpsed as present in the humiliating beginning.

Like the radiant blackness of the Kaaba cloth, Sufis adore the darkness of the deep of night when conversation with the divine is easiest. Perhaps it's that engendering black that's felt in these opening pages.

**W**HAT
STRANGE
BEINGS
WE ARE!
THAT SITTING
IN HELL
AT THE
BOTTOM
OF THE DARK,
WE'RE AFRAID
OF OUR OWN

IMMORTALITY.

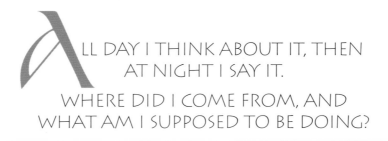

# ALL DAY I THINK ABOUT IT, THEN AT NIGHT I SAY IT.

## WHERE DID I COME FROM, AND WHAT AM I SUPPOSED TO BE DOING?

I HAVE NO IDEA

## MY SOUL IS FROM ELSEWHERE, I'M SURE OF THAT,

and I intend to end up there.
This drunkeness began
in some other tavern.
When I get back around
to that place, I'll  be
completely sober. Meanwhile,
I'm like a bird from another
continent, sitting in this aviary.
The day is coming when I fly off,
but who is it now in my ear,
who hears my voice?
Who says words with my mouth?

Who looks out with my eyes?
What is the soul?
I cannot stop asking.
If I could taste one sip
of an answer, I could break out
of this prison for drunks.

I didn't come here of my own accord,
and I can't leave that way.

Whoever brought me here
will have to take me home.

**S**OMETIMES
I FORGET COMPLETELY
WHAT COMPANIONSHIP IS.
Unconscious and insane
I spill sad energy
everywhere. My story
gets told in various ways:
a romance, a dirty joke,
a war, a vacancy.
Divide up my
forgetfulness
to any number,
it will go around.

These dark suggestions
that I follow,
are they part
of some plan?

Friends,
be careful.
Don't
come near me
out of curiosity,
or sympathy.

**A** BLACK SKY
HATES
THE MOON.
I am that dark
nothing. I hate those
in power.
I'm invited in from the
road to the house
but I invent some excuse.
Now I'm angry
at the road.
I don't need love. Let
someone break me.
I don't want
to hear anyone's
trouble. I've had my
chance for wealth
and position.
I don't want those.
I am iron resisting
the most enormous
magnet there is.

In
# Complete Control,
## -Pretending Control.
### With dignified authority,

*We are charlatans...*

Or maybe just a goat's-hair brush in a painter's hand.

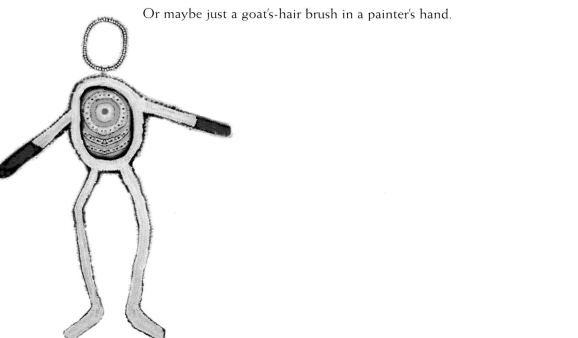

WE HAVE NO IDEA WHAT WE ARE.

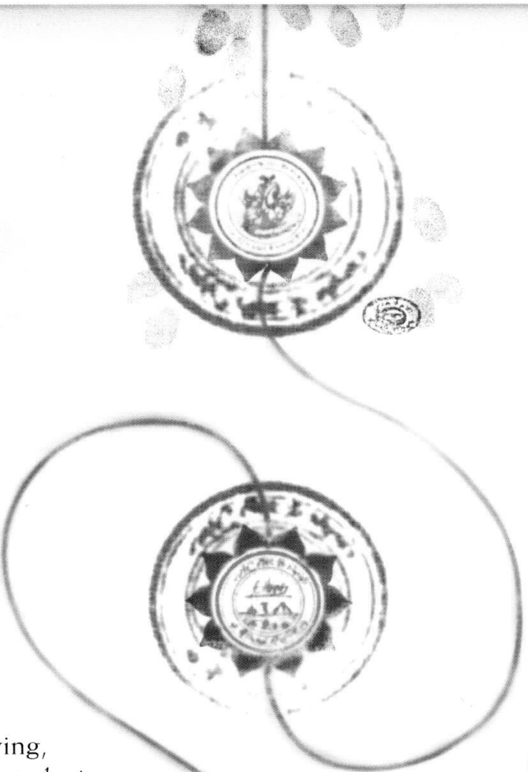

You
  sit here
    for days saying,
      *This is strange business.*
You're the strange business. You
have the energy of the sun in you,
but you keep knotting it up
at the base of your spine.

You're some weird kind of gold
that wants to stay melted
in the furnace, so you won't have to
become coins.

Say ONE in your lonesome house.
Loving all the rest is hiding
inside a lie.

You've
  gotten
    drunk
on so many kinds of wine.
Taste this. It won't
make you wild.
      It's fire. Give up,
if you don't understand
by this time
that your living is firewood.

This wave of talking
builds. Better
we should not speak,
      but let it grow within.

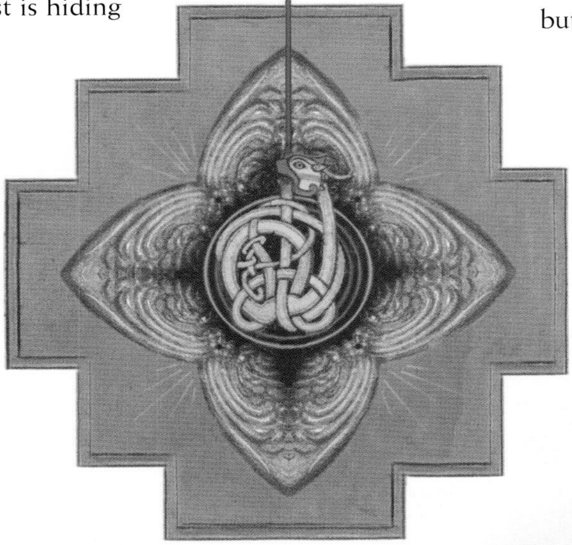

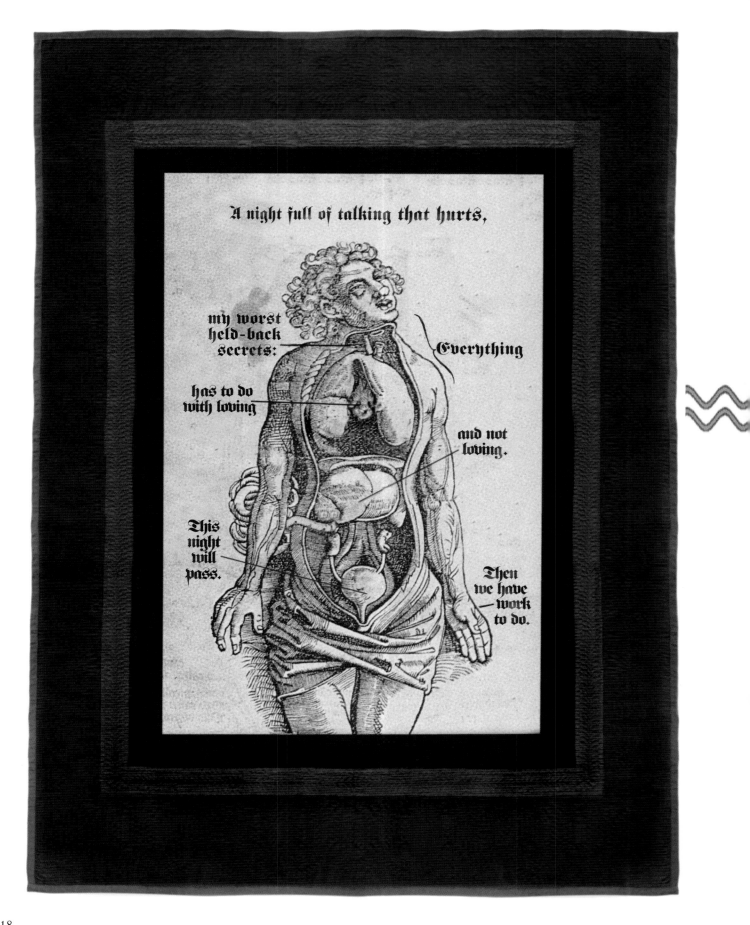

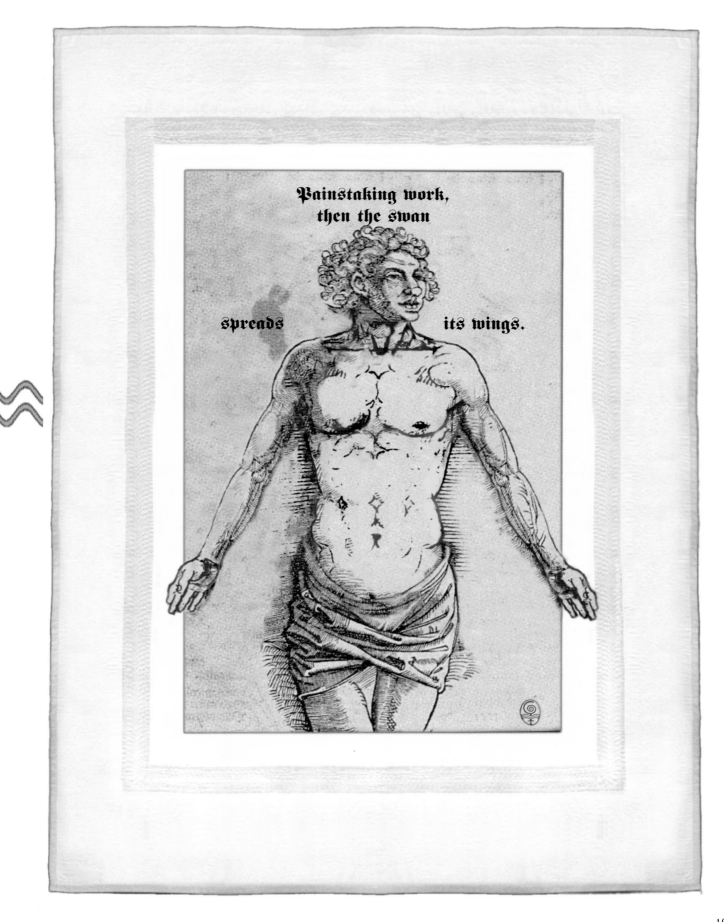

Painstaking work,
then the swan

spreads                    its wings.

Y ou miss the garden
because you want a small fig
from a random tree.
You don't meet
the beautiful woman.
You're joking with an old crone.

It makes me want to cry
how she detains you,
stinking–mouthed, with a hundred
talons, putting her head
over the roof edge to call down,
tasteless fig, fold over fold, empty
as dry-rotten garlic.

She has you by the belt,
even though there's no flower
and no milk inside her body.

Death will open your eyes
to what her face is. Leather spine
of a black lizard.

NO
MORE
ADVICE

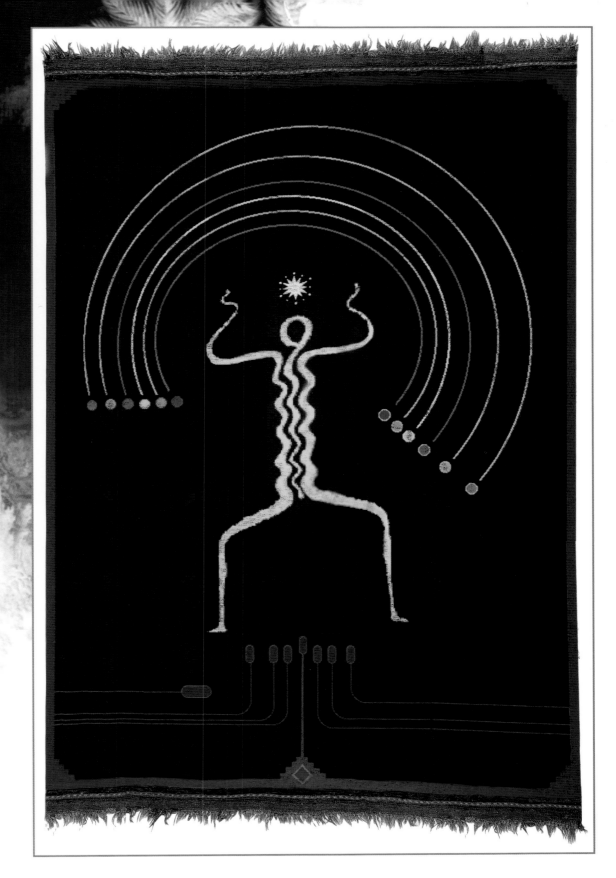

LET YOURSELF BE SILENTLY DRAWN
BY THE STRONGER PULL
OF WHAT YOU REALLY LOVE.

# RISE UP NIMBLY & GO ON YOUR STRANGE JOURNEY

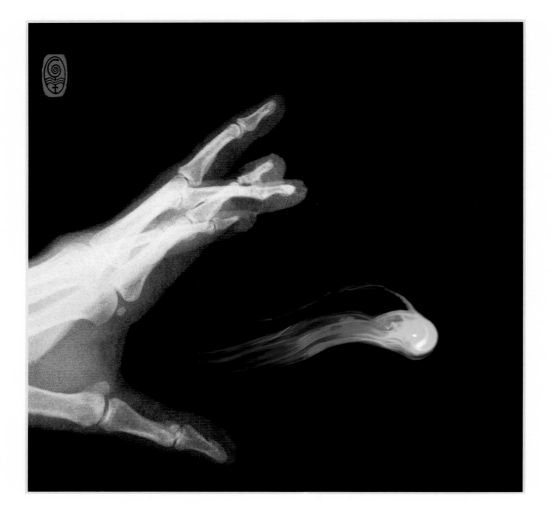

## THE REAL WORK

There is one thing in this world that you must never forget to do. If you forget everything else and not this, there's nothing to worry about; but if you remember everything else and forget this, then you will have done nothing in your life.

It's as if a king has sent you to some country to do a task, and you perform a hundred other services, but not the one he sent you to do. So human beings come to this world to do particular work. That work is the purpose, and each is specific to the person. If you don't do it, it's as though a priceless Indian sword were used to slice rotten meat. It's a golden bowl being used to cook turnips, when one filing from the bowl could buy a hundred suitable pots. It's a knife of the finest tempering nailed into a wall to hang things on.

You say, "But look, I'm using the dagger. It's not lying idle."

Do you hear how ludicrous that sounds? For a penny, an iron nail could be bought to serve the purpose. You say, "But I spend my energies on lofty enterprises. I study jurisprudence and philosophy and logic and astronomy and medicine and all the rest." But consider why you do those things. They are all branches of yourself.

Remember the deep root of your being, the presence of your lord. Give your life to the one who already owns your breath and your moments. If you don't, you will be exactly like the man who takes a precious dagger and hammers it into his kitchen wall for a peg to hold his dipper gourd. You'll be wasting valuable keenness and foolishly ignoring your dignity and your purpose.

–Rumi

# THE PROPHETS

have wondered to themselves,
"How long
should we keep pounding this
cold iron? How long
do we have to whisper into an empty cage?"

So don't be timid.
Load the ship and set out.

No one knows for certain
whether the vessel will sink
or reach the harbor.

Just don't be one of those merchants
who won't risk the ocean!

This is much more important
than losing or making money!

This is your connection to God.

Think of the fear and the hope that you have
about your livelihood. They make you
go to work diligently every day.

Now consider what
the prophets have done.
Abraham wore fire
for an anklet.

Moses spoke to the sea.
David moulded iron.
Solomon rode the wind.

Work in the invisible world
at least as hard
as you do in the visible.

Be a companion with the prophets,
invisibly, so that no one knows.

You can't imagine what profit will come!
When one of those generous ones
invites you into his fire,
go quickly!
Don't say,
"But will it burn me?
Will it hurt?"

Rise! Move around the center
as pilgrims wind the Kaaba.

Being still is how one clay clod
sticks to another in sleep,

while movement wakes us up
and unlocks
new blessings.

Rise up nimbly
and go on your strange journey
to the ocean of meanings.

The stream knows
it can't stay on the mountain.
Leave  and don't look away
from the sun as you go,
in whose light
you're sometimes crescent,
sometimes full.

Can you endure silence?
Are you a night fighter?

Or more a child bored
with outgrown toys
trying to win at
tip-the-cat?

If you have any patience
left, *we* know what to do.

If you love sleep,
we'll tear you away.
If you change into a mountain,
we'll melt you.

If you become an ocean,
*we'll drain you.*

# THIS IS HOW A HUMAN BEING CAN CHANGE:

There's a worm addicted to eating
grape leaves.
     Suddenly, he wakes up,
call it grace, whatever, something
wakes him, and he's no longer
a worm.

He's the entire vineyard,
and the orchard too,
the fruit, the trunks,
a growing wisdom and joy
that doesn't need
to devour.

# LOVERS THINK THEY'RE LOOKING FOR EACH OTHER, BUT THERE'S ONLY ONE SEARCH: WANDERING THIS WORLD

## IS WANDERING THAT,

both inside one
transparent sky. In here
there is no dogma and no heresy.

The miracle of Jesus is himself, not
what he said or did
about the future. Forget the future.
I'd worship someone who could do that!

On the way you may want to look back, or not,

but if you can say There's nothing ahead,
there will be nothing there.

Stretch your arms and take hold the cloth of your clothes
with both hands. The cure for pain is in the pain.
Good and bad are mixed. If you don't have both,
you don't belong with us.

When one of us gets lost, is not here, he must be inside us.
There's no place like that anywhere in the world.

# DON'T GO ANYWHERE WITHOUT ME.

LET NOTHING HAPPEN IN THE SKY OR ON THE GROUND,
IN THIS WORLD OR THAT WORLD,
WITHOUT MY BEING IN ITS HAPPENING.

Vision, see nothing I don't see.
Language, say nothing.
The way the night
knows itself with the moon,
be that way with me.
Be the rose
nearest to the thorn that I am.
I want to feel myself in you
when you taste food, in the arc
of your mallet when you work.
When you visit friends,
when you go up on the roof
by yourself at night.
There's nothing worse
than to walk out
along the street without you.
I don't know where I'm going.
You're the road
and the knower of roads,
more than maps,
more than love.

L
    isten to  the story told by the reed
of being separated.

Since I was cut from the reed bed
I have made
this crying sound. Anyone
separated from someone he loves
understands what I say:

> Anyone pulled
>     from a source
>         longs to go back.

At any gathering I am there,
mingling in the laughing
and the grieving, a friend
to each.

But few will hear the secrets
    hidden
        within
            the
                notes.
No ears for that.
Body flowing
    out of Spirit.
Spirit flowing
    from body.

No concealing that mixing,
But it's not given us
    to see the soul.

The reed flute is fire, not wind.
                    Be that empty.

Hear the love-fire tangled in the notes
as bewilderment melts into wine.

This reed is a friend to all
who want the fabric torn
and drawn away.

The reed is hurt and salve combining.
Intimacy
and longing for intimacy, one song.
    A disasterous surrender
                and a fine love, together.

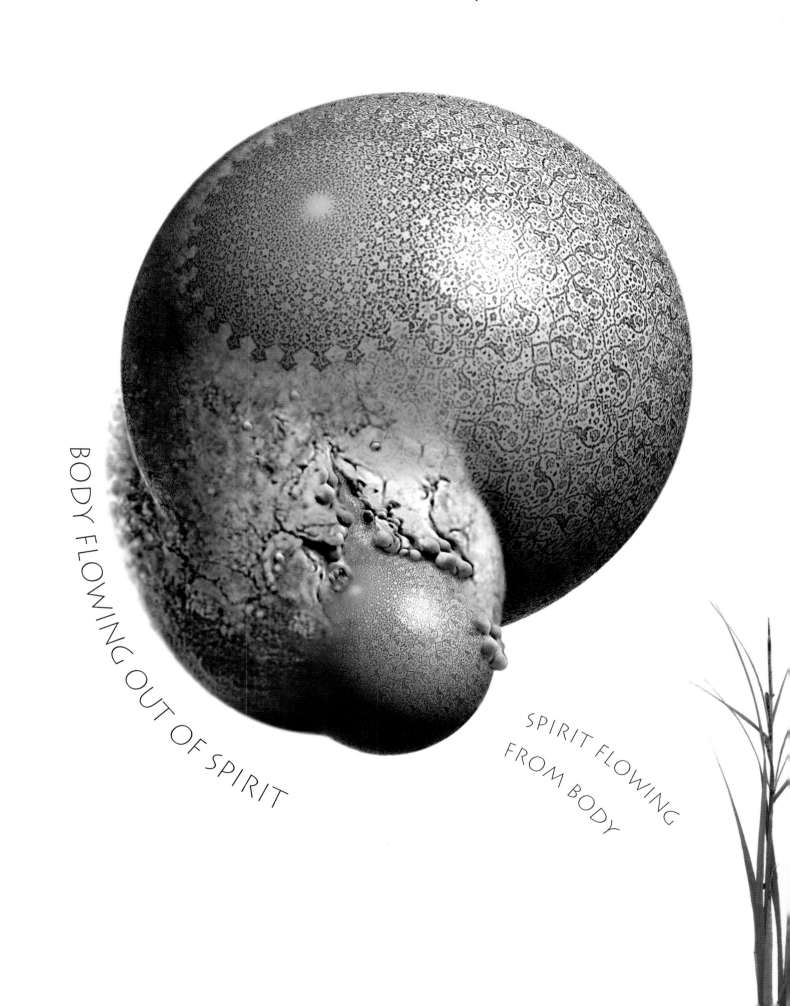

BODY FLOWING OUT OF SPIRIT

SPIRIT FLOWING FROM BODY

# COME TO THE ORCHARD

(THESE DO NOT MATTER)

In Rumi's poetry, the orchard is an emblem of the sacred imagination, the place where knots are untied. It is a call to move within, but not reactively; not curling up like a dog in the cold, but soaring inward like an eagle.

What may seem at first to be an emptiness of no consolations, no desire, a grand aloneness, becomes garden-like. You walk the open-roofed sanctuary, between the lines of trees, rabbits in the aisles.

The orchard is the place where the heart opens. It might be a bridge into meditation, or a visit to a learning community like the one Rumi presided over. Much of his poetry can be heard as a friendly invitation. He tries to catch us where we are. A man talking to his barber. The taste of cabbage broth. The joy of skin contact. The fascination of haggling over a price. Painting delicate persimmons with a goat's-hair brush. Anything human beings do, every story, can serve for Rumi as a lens to see the growth of the soul. Whatever curl of hair interests you, he uses that to draw you to the greater whole.

The Indian master Ramakrishna was once approached by someone who said, "I'd like to bring my cousin to see you, but he's not interested."

Ramakrishna replied, "Tell him we have fish soup."

KEEP WALKING, THOUGH THERE'S NO PLACE TO GET TO.

DON'T TRY TO SEE THROUGH

THE DISTANCES.

THAT'S NOT FOR

HUMAN BEINGS.

MOVE

WITHIN,

BUT DON'T

MOVE THE WAY

FEAR

MAKES

YOU

MOVE.

Today, like every other day, we wake up empty
and frightened. Don't open the door to the study
and begin reading. Take down a musical instrument.

Let the beauty we love be what we do.
There are hundreds of ways to kneel and kiss the ground.

baby pigeon stands on the edge of a nest all day.
Then he hears a whistle, Come to me.
How could he not fly toward that?
Wings tear through the body's robe
when the letter arrives
that says,

        "You've flapped and fluttered against limits
long enough.

You've been a bird without wings in a house without doors
or windows.

Compassion builds a door.
Restlessness cuts a key.

Step off
proudly into sunlight,
not looking back.

Take sips of this pure wine being poured.
Don't mind that you've been given a dirty cup."

**T**HOSE WHO DON'T FEEL THIS

LOVE

PULLING

THEM

LIKE A RIVER,

those
who don't drink dawn
like a cup of springwater
or take in sunset
like supper,
those who don't
want to change,
let them sleep.

This love
is beyond the study of theology,
that old trickery and hypocrisy.
If you want to improve your mind
that way, sleep on.

I've given up on my brain,
I've torn the cloth to shreds
and thrown it away. If you're not
completely naked, wrap
your beautiful robe of words
around you,

AND SLEEP.

33

COME

TO THE ORCHARD IN SPRING.

THERE IS LIGHT AND WINE AND

SWEETHEARTS IN THE POMEGRANATE

FLOWERS.

IF YOU DO NOT COME, THESE DO NOT

MATTER.

IF YOU DO COME, THESE DO NOT MATTER.

There's a strange
frenzy in my head,
of birds flying,
each particle
circulating on its own.
Is the one I love
everywhere?

 HAVE LIVED

ON THE LIP OF

INSANITY, WANTING TO

KNOW REASONS, KNOCKING

ON A DOOR.

I T OPENS.

I'VE BEEN KNOCKING FROM THE INSIDE!

# THERE IS A BREATHING

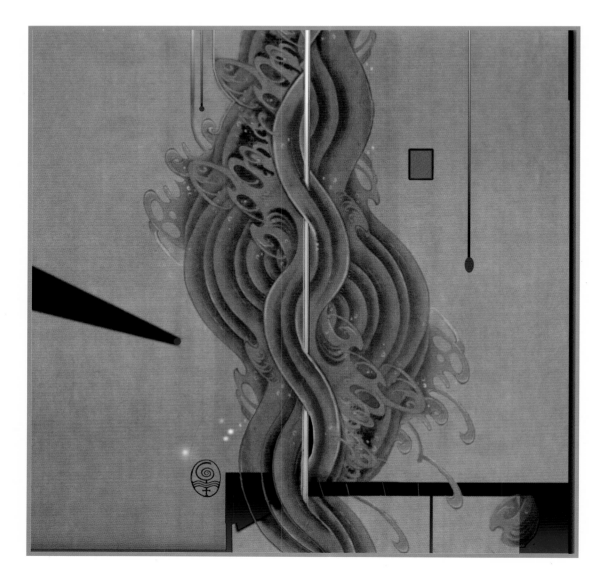

## ELEGANCE

It's a common thing to hear in kitchens now, or anywhere where household discussions are going on, "Breathe. Wait a minute. Just breathe."

We all know that things get better when we pay attention to the breath. We're more in the moment, more present, more true.

There are things to do. Enlightenment unfolds as it will, but there are ways to become more accessible to it.

Practices. Meditation. Vigils. Fasting. Walks. Whatever you give time and attention to. Rumi says it's important to *relish* these doings. As work becomes play, breath easier, the weaving becomes elegant.

In the rhythm of a practice, life begins to fit together at the water table level. You feel the artistry moving through a web of conduits.

Conventionally, we think of repetition as deadening, but in a spiritual practice, repetition, *done with delight*, renews the freshness, the originality, the brightness of spontaneity. Doing some awareness work regularly sharpens the *point*, makes inner life more beautiful, and that beauty revives.

$\mathcal{A}$n eye is meant to see things.

The soul

is here
for its own joy.

A head
has one use: for loving a true love.

Legs: to run after.
Love is for vanishing into the sky. The mind,
for learning what men have done and tried to do.
Mysteries are not to be solved.
The eye goes blind
when it only wants to see *why*.
A lover is always accused of something.
But when he finds his love, whatever was lost
in the looking comes back completely changed.
On the way to Mecca, many
dangers: thieves,
the blowing sand, only camel's milk to drink.
Still, each pilgrim kisses the black stone there
with pure longing, feeling in the surface
the taste of the lips he wants.

This talk is like stamping new coins.
They pile up,
while the real work is being done outside
by someone digging in the ground.

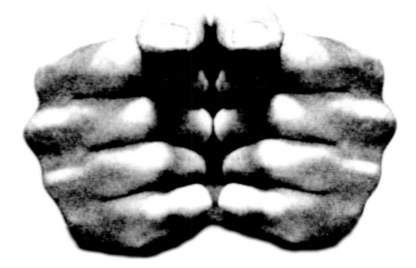

*T*HERE IS A WAY
OF BREATHING

THAT'S A SHAME AND A SUFFOCATION

AND THERE'S ANOTHER WAY OF EXPIRING,
A LOVE BREATH,

THAT LETS YOU OPEN INFINITELY.

It has been suggested by some scientists that the primeval tidal rhythms that nurtured our genetic ancestors in some distant epoch have left, even now, a faint imprint on our body's biorhythms. The teachings of the Sufis suggest that there is a deeper, more profound pulse and flow operating in creation that we move to. This is the love-breath of Jelaluddin's poem, and it is the core of a teaching-practice. All traditions recognize an eternal ebb and flow that is intimately connected with the breath. When we bring a conscious connection to this inner tide we connect with the Whole. The practice is deceptively simple. Gentle attention is paid to the breath. No attempt at all is made to control it, but rather only to observe it in its most natural and relaxed state. With every out-breath is visualized a discharging of all desire-grasping, aching, neurosis, muddiness of mind, obsession— all the strategies the illusory "I" uses to maintain its tenuous sense of separation. This discharging is felt as a cleansing, beginning at our furthest extremities moving through subtle nerve channels, flowing through and clearing the heart, and out the left nostril. To focus the mind, the revealing phrase *La illaha* can silently accompany this movement—or its most profound English equivalent,

THE "I" IS AN ILLUSION.

The in-breath is witnessed as a radiant Presence entering the right nostril, spreading upwards first to the mystical Sight center between the eyebrows (the *Kursh*, in Sufi nomenclature) continuing upwards to a golden crown of light at the top of the head (the *Arsh*), and finally dropping to its seat in the center of the heart, the Noor. The accompanying thought-pattern is *Il' Allahu*, or

GOD ALONE IS REAL

# N

OT
CHRISTIAN OR JEW OR
MUSLIM, NOT HINDU,
BUDDHIST, SUFI, OR ZEN.
NOT ANY RELIGION

OR CULTURAL SYSTEM. I AM
NOT FROM THE EAST
OR THE WEST, NOT
OUT OF THE OCEAN OR UP

FROM THE GROUND, NOT
NATURAL OR ETHEREAL, NOT
COMPOSED OF ELEMENTS AT ALL.
I DO NOT EXIST,

AM NOT AN ENTITY IN THIS
WORLD OR THE NEXT,
DID NOT DESCEND FROM
ADAM AND EVE OR ANY

ORIGIN STORY. MY PLACE IS
THE PLACELESS, A TRACE
OF THE TRACELESS.
NEITHER BODY OR SOUL.

I BELONG TO THE BELOVED,
HAVE SEEN THE TWO
WORLDS AS ONE AND
THAT ONE
CALL TO AND KNOW,

FIRST, LAST, OUTER, INNER,
ONLY THAT BREATH BREATHING

# HUMAN BEING.

In the early morning hour, just before dawn, lover and Beloved wake and take a drink of water.

SHE ASKS, "DO YOU LOVE ME OR YOURSELF MORE?
REALLY, TELL THE ABSOLUTE TRUTH."

He says, "There's nothing left of me.
I'm like a ruby held up to the sunrise.
Is it still a stone, or a world
made of redness?"

This is how Hallaj said, *I am God*
and told the truth!

The ruby and the sunrise are one.
Be courageous and discipline yourself.

Completely become hearing and ear
and wear this sun-ruby as an earring.

Work. Keep digging your well.
Don't think about getting off from work.
Water is there somewhere.

Submit to a daily practice.
Your loyalty to that
is a ring on the door.

Keep knocking, and the joy inside
will eventually open a window
and look out to see who's there.

Roar

YOU THAT COME TO BIRTH

AND BRING THE MYSTERIES,

YOUR VOICE-THUNDER

MAKES US VERY HAPPY.

ROAR, LION OF THE HEART,

**AND TEAR ME OPEN.**

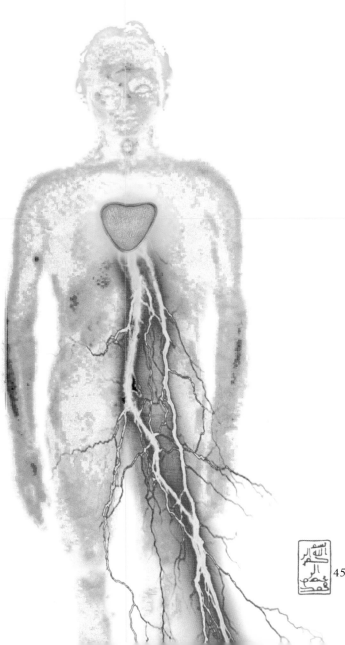

There's a hidden sweetness
in the stomach's emptiness.
We are lutes, no more, no less. If the soundbox
is stuffed full of anything, no music.
If the brain and the belly are burning clean
with fasting, every moment a new song comes
out of the fire. The fog clears, and a new energy
makes you run up the steps in front of you.
Be emptier and cry like reed instruments cry.
Emptier, write secrets with the reed pen.
When you're full of food and drink, Satan sits
where your spirit should, an ugly metal statue
in place of the Kaaba. When you fast,
good habits gather like friends who want to help.
Fasting is Soloman's ring. Don't give it
to some illusion and lose your power.
But even if you've lost all will and control,
they come back when you fast, like soldiers appearing
out of the ground, pennants flying above them.

A table descends to your tents,
Jesus' table.
Expect to see it, when you fast, this table
spread with other food better
than the broth of cabbages.

## Bend, Tend, Disappear

This is how you change
when you go to the orchard
where the heart opens:

you become
fragrance and the light
that burning oil gives off,

long strands of grieving hair, lion
and at the same time, gazelle.

You're walking alone without feet,
as riverwater does.

The taste of a wine that is bitter and sweet,
seen and unseen, neither wet nor dry,
like Jesus reaching to touch.

A new road appears without desirous imagining,
inside God's breath,

empty, where you quit saying
the name and there's no distance,
no calling dove-coo.

A window, a wild rose at the field's edge,
you'll be me,
but don't feel proud or happy.

Bend like the limb of a peach tree.
Tend those who need help.
Disappear three days with the moon.

Don't pray to be healed, or look for evidence
of "some other world."
You are the soul
and medicine for what wounds the soul.

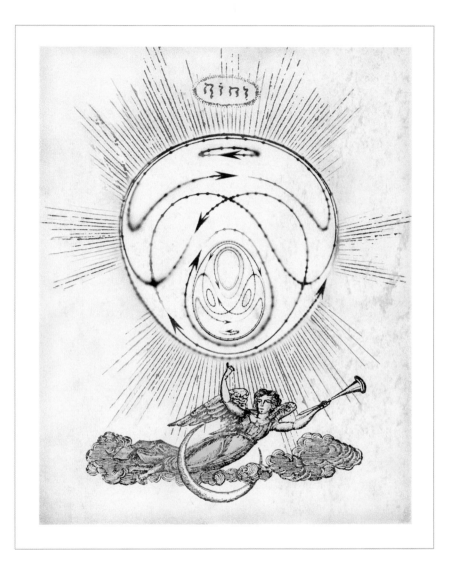

A new moon teaches gradualness
and deliberation and how one gives birth
to oneself slowly. Patience with small details
makes perfect a large work, like the universe.

What nine months of attention does for an embryo
forty early mornings will do
for your gradually growing wholeness.

Muhammad says,
"I come before sunrise
to chain you and drag you off."
It's amazing, and funny, that you have to be pulled away
from being tortured, pulled out
into this Spring garden,
                          but that's the way it is.

Almost everyone must be bound and dragged here.
Only a few come on their own.

Children have to be made to go to school at first.
Then some of them begin to like it.
                          They run to school.
They expand with the learning.
                          Later, they receive money
because of something they've learned at school,
and they get really excited, awake all night,
as watchful and alive as thieves!

Some nights stay up till dawn
as the moon sometimes does
for the sun.
Be a full bucket pulled up
the dark way
of a well, then lifted
out into light.

Stars burn clear
all night.

Do that yourself, and a spring
will rise in the dark with water
your deepest thirst is for.

This night there are
no limits
to what may be given.

This is not a night but
a marriage,

a couple whispering in bed in
unison
the same words.

Darkness simply lets down a
curtain for that.

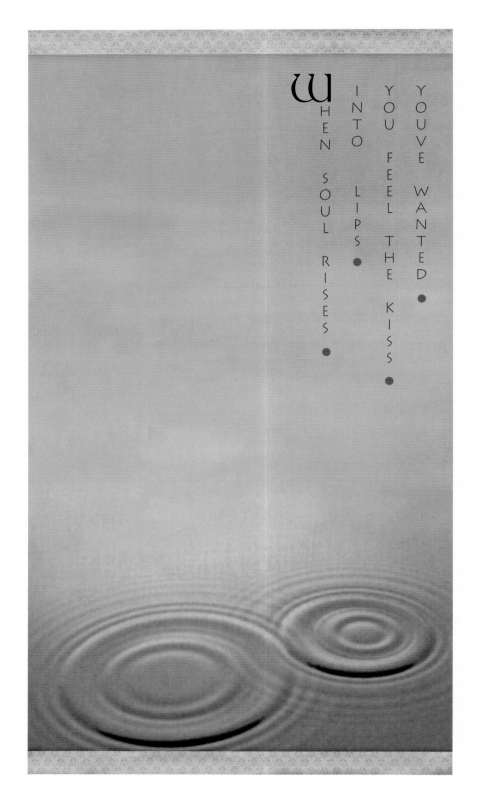

When soul rises • into lips • you feel the kiss • you've wanted •

oul:

*where this tree grows and learns
to drink without getting drunk.
Soul soaks into existence everywhere,
except my rough, contemptuous
personality.*

riend:

*intelligence,
sometimes the soul,*

*water, bread, a cave
where we sit with friends,*

*invisible bowl to drink from,
health coming back to a patient,*

*definite statement, pulsing spring,
cloud, I'll stop,*

*not because
words have become tedious,
but to keep that bird sitting on its branch.*

## THE FRIEND

Who is the Friend, the Beloved, the *you* Rumi speaks of and to? An expansiveness felt inside a presence. The one who reads the book of the universe.

It could also be said that the Friend is Rumi's way of referring to the core impulse in the psyche that generates religions and remains beyond the divisions they incur.

Sufis say the clearest connection to God is inside the heart. When you move more and more into that love center, the ache of being two, of feeling separation, dissolves. Rumi speaks of "polishing the mirror of the heart." Less esoterically, whatever is deeply loved—friend, granddaughter, late afternoon light, masonry, tennis, whatever absorbs you—this may be a reflection of how you move in the invisible world of spirit. It might be several months of moving rocks and building stone steps. It might be tending a garden, or fixing a sink. It is your beauty, the elegant point where everything is one. Sufis call it the *qalb.*

The *unio mystica* is a lived thing, not a theological concept. It's a transformed intention, an intensity, and the peace of walking inside it: the Friend.

The poem above, without being theological, or logical, refines the *Friend* and *soul* as terms, yet leaves them in *this* moment, bird on branch.

IN ANY GATHERING, IN ANY
CHANCE MEETING
ON THE STREET, THERE IS
A SHINE, AN ELEGANCE

RISING

UP

TODAY, I RECOGNIZED THAT THE JEWEL-LIKE BEAUTY
IS THE PRESENCE,

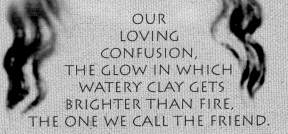

OUR
LOVING
CONFUSION,
THE GLOW IN WHICH
WATERY CLAY GETS
BRIGHTER THAN FIRE,
THE ONE WE CALL THE FRIEND.

I BEGGED, "IS THERE A WAY INTO YOU, A LADDER?"

"YOUR HEAD
IS THE LADDER,
BRING IT DOWN UNDER YOUR FEET."

THE MIND, THIS GLOBE OF AWARENESS, IS A STARRY UNIVERSE THAT WHEN YOU PUSH OFF WITH
YOUR FOOT,
A THOUSAND NEW ROADS
BECOME CLEAR,
AS YOU YOURSELF DO
AT DAWN, SAILING
THROUGH
THE LIGHT.

# l WOULD LOVE  TO KISS YOU

THE PRICE OF KISSING IS YOUR LIFE.

Now my loving is running toward my life
shouting

WHAT A BARGAIN! LET'S BUY IT.

GAMBLE
EVERYTHING
FOR
LOVE,

IF YOU'RE
A TRUE
HUMAN
BEING

IF NOT, LEAVE        THIS GATHERING

Half-heartedness doesn't reach into majesty. You set out to find God, but then you keep
stopping for long periods
at meanspirited roadhouses.

# ᴅON'T WAIT
# ANY LONGER.

D
I
V
E

IN
THE OCEAN,
LEAVE
& LET THE SEA
BE YOU.
Silent, absent,
walking
an empty road,
*all praise.*

I
you
he
she
we...

IN THE GARDEN OF MYSTIC
LOVERS, THESE
ARE NOT
TRUE
DISTINCTIONS.

It's the old rule that drunks
  have to argue
and get into fights.
The lover is just as bad:
he falls into a hole.
But down in that hole he finds
something shining,
worth more than any amount
of money or power.
Last night the moon came
dropping her clothes
in the street.
I took it as a sign to start singing,
falling up into the bowl of sky.
The bowl breaks.
Everywhere is falling
everywhere.

Nothing else to do.

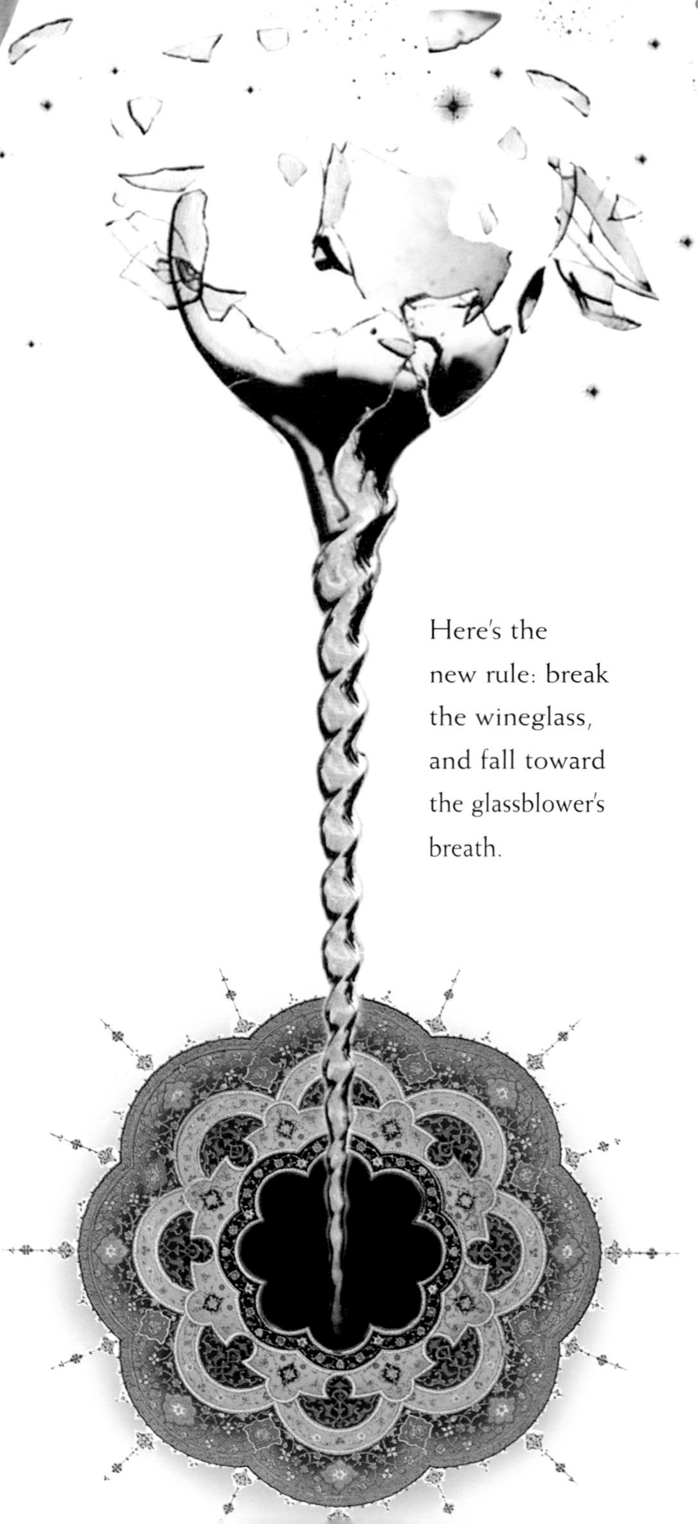

Here's the
new rule: break
the wineglass,
and fall toward
the glassblower's
breath.

LATE, BY MYSELF, IN THE
BOAT OF MYSELF,
NO LIGHT AND NO LAND
ANYWHERE,
CLOUDCOVER THICK.
I TRY TO STAY
JUST ABOVE THE SURFACE,

YET I'M ALREADY UNDER
AND LIVING
-
WITHIN


THE   OCEAN.

No one knows what makes the soul
wake up so happy!

Maybe a dawn breeze has blown the veil
from the face of God.

A thousand new moons appear.
Roses open laughing.

Hearts become perfect rubies
like those from Badakshan.

The body turns entirely spirit.
Leaves become branches in this wind!

Why is it now so easy to surrender,
even for those already surrendered?

There's no answer to any of this.
No one knows the source of joy.

A poet breathes into a reed flute,
and the tip of every hair makes music.

Shams sails down clods of dirt
from the roof,

and we take jobs
as doorkeepers for him.

You are the
taste in
every lip,
the intention
of every religion,
you swing

your great heart out

of the ground
and put your shapes
in the air.

Half crazy
is not nearly enough
for you!
The sacred letter *alif*

turns into a circle, the rim
of a wineglass.

This madness rises
out of love, and weeping.

We must not be afraid of
what anyone might say:

B E   S O U R C E ,   N O T   R E S U L T .

*Gone, inner and outer,*
*no moon, no ground or sky.*
*Don't hand me another glass of wine.*
*Pour it into my mouth.*
*I've lost the way to my mouth.*

There are wild
wandering sufis
called *qalandars,*
who are constantly tickled
with life.

It's scandalous how they love
and laugh at any small event.

People gossip about them,
and that makes them deft
in their cunning, but really
a great God-wrestling goes on
inside these wanderers, a flood of sunlight
that's drunk with the whole thing.

Someone's putting a spell on me,
another expects me to repent,
another runs alongside without feet!
Drunk inside the whole thing.

Friends rush out in the rain
to be soaked with the sky.

Eyesight holding understanding,
the moon's polite manner.

Tell the soldier about to go to war
how the cypress tree is turning
green, drunk with the forest.

A country with no roads or religions
could possibly be...drunk
with the whole thing.

Someone beyond questions of how
and what for sews patches
on my robe, someone who watches

the sea, Mt. Sinai and Friend,
that one comes whispering, Be
drunk with the whole thing.

Tell the festival of sacrifice,
tell the Qur'an, tell the gate of heaven,
there's a bunch out here singing
and drunk with the whole.

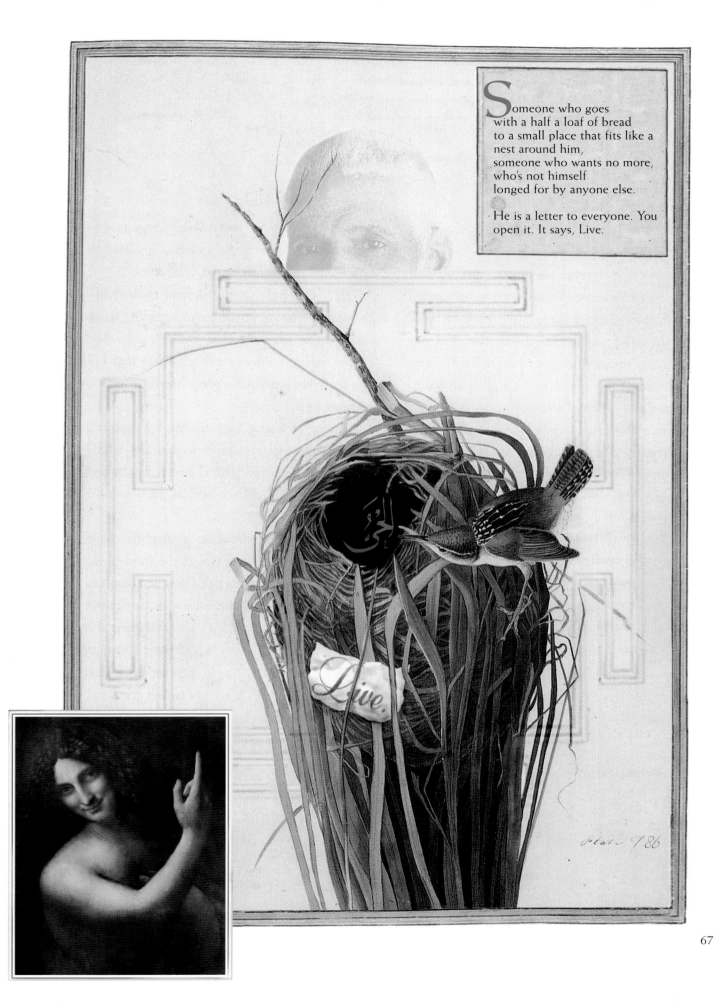

Someone who goes
with a half a loaf of bread
to a small place that fits like a
nest around him,
someone who wants no more,
who's not himself
longed for by anyone else.

He is a letter to everyone. You
open it. It says, Live.

67

I say these things disinterestedly.
Accept them in kind.

## LOVE IS A MADMAN, WORKING HIS WILD SCHEMES,

tearing off his clothes,
running through the
mountains, drinking poison,
and now quietly choosing
annihilation.

There are love stories,
and there is obliteration into love.
You've been walking
the ocean's edge, holding
up your robes to keep them dry.
You must dive naked under,
   and deeper
      under, a thousand times deeper!

Love flows down.
The ground submits
to the sky,
and suffers what comes.

Tell me, is the earth worse
for giving in like that?

Don't put blankets over the drum!
Open completely.

Let your spirit ear listen
to the green dome's
passionate murmur.

# ꙨEAR DOWN THIS HOUSE.

A hundred thousand new houses can be built
from the transparent yellow carnelian buried beneath

and the only way to get to that
is to do the work of demolishing and then

digging under the foundation. With that value
in hand all the new construction will be done

without effort. And anyway, sooner or later this house
will fall on its own. The jewel treasure will be

uncovered, but it won't be yours then. The buried
wealth is your pay for doing the demolition,

the pick and the shovel work. If you wait and just
let it happen, you'll bite your hand and say,

"I didn't do as I knew I should have." This
is a rented house. You don't own the deed.

You have a lease, and you've set up a little shop,
where you barely make a living sewing patches

on torn clothing. Yet only a few feet underneath
are two veins, pure red and bright gold carnelian.

Take the pickaxe and pry the foundation.
You've got to quit this seamstress work.

What does the patch-sewing mean you ask? Eating
and drinking.  The heavy cloak of the body

is always getting torn. You patch it with food
and other restless ego-satisfactions. Rip up

one board from the shop floor and look into
the basement. You'll see two glints in the dirt.

The house that must be torn down is the false ego structure,
the identity overlaid by culture, and the soap-opera self of
what you think you want. The pickax of fierce attention-
work dismantles this illusion, and discovers the treasure that
is beyond experience, the jewel lights of our other eyes. The
hidden treasure image contains a beautiful Islamic cosmolo-
gy: God created the universe because he wanted to be
known. Rumi's commentary is that when human beings do
their pickax work, that happens!

THIS IS HOW I WOULD DIE
INTO THE LOVE
I HAVE FOR YOU:

AS PIECES OF CLOUD

DISSOLVE

IN

SUNLIGHT

# THE PATH OF BLAME

## THE HURT WE EMBRACE

Being near the splendor is unhinging. The path of love-surrender can bring about a frenzy to be broken open, emptied out, burned to a crisp, a desperate honesty that has only one conclusion: *guilty as charged*. "Everyone's scandalous flaw is mine."

It takes a moth-mind courage to fly into the flames.

The Way of Blame is not a matter of journeying home. At this point it's dreg drinking and desolation, and a hurrying to have the false ego structure torn down to bedrock.

Shams seems to wander this territory. He comes from no conventional lineage. His was the nomadic way of a reckless *qalandar*. To these wanderers every chance meeting gives a taste of the mystery.

Shams once said that Rumi wrote in three scripts: one that only he (Rumi) could read, one that he and everyone else could read, and one that neither Rumi nor anyone else could read. *I am that third script,* said Shams.

Shams is the sun, that admits no metaphor for itself, an unreadable book. The Friend who advises: *Be notorious. You've tried prudent planning long enough.* Shams once said that if you lifted the Kaaba up, everyone would see that what we're really worshipping is each other—the shared essence which is most clearly seen in the human face.

Rumi, Shams, and Khidr, the guide of souls, were grounded in action, the work that breaks us open and devastates the habitual self. Shams' way of changing is *specific*, and difficult, like plowing a field. It does not involve "flying off to blue perfection." These beings go back past the origin of religions to the impulse of wonder and recognition that drew a hand on a cave wall.

That hurt we embrace becomes joy.
Call it to your arms where it can change.
A silkworm eating leaves makes a cocoon.
Each of us weaves a chamber
of leaves and sticks.
Like silkworms, we begin to exist
as we disappear
inside that room.

Without legs, we fly.
When I stop speaking, this poem
will close in silence more magnificent....

I don't regret how much I love,
and I avoid those who repent their passion.

Hundreds of sweethearts!
I am the lover and the one
lovers long for.  Blue, and a cure
for blues, sky in a small cage,

badly hurt but flying.
Everybody's scandalous flaw is mine.

73

A man was breaking up the soil,
when another man came by, "Why
are you ruining this land?"

"Don't be a fool! Nothing can
grow until the ground
is turned over and crumbled.

There can be no roses
and no orchard
without first this that looks devastating.

You must lance an ulcer to heal it.
You must tear down parts of an old building
to restore it, and so it is with a sensual life
that has no spirit in it.
                    To change,
a person must face the dragon of his appetites
with another dragon, the life-energy
of the soul."
                    When that's not strong,
the world seems to be full of people
who have your own fears and wantings.

As one thinks the room is spinning
when he's whirling around.

When your love contracts in anger,
the atmosphere itself feels threatening

But when you're expansive, no matter
what the weather, you're in an open,
windy field with friends.

Many people travel to Syria and Iraq
and meet only hypocrites.

Others go all the way to India
and see just merchants buying and selling.

Others go to Turkestan and China
and find those countries filled
with sneak-thieves and cheats.

We always see the qualities
that are living in us.

A cow may walk from one side of the amazing city
of Baghdad to the other and notice only
a watermelon rind and a tuft of hay
that fell off a wagon.

Don't keep repeatedly doing
what your animal-soul wants to do.
That's like deciding to be a strip of meat
nailed and drying on a board in the sun.

Your spirit needs to follow the changes happening
in the spacious place it knows about.

There, the scene is always new,
a clairvoyant river of picturing,
more beautiful than any on earth.

This is where the sufis wash.
Purify your eyes, and see the pure world.
Your life will fill with radiant forms.

IT'S A QUESTION OF CLEANING
THEN DEVELOPING.
SPIRITUAL SENSES!

See

BEYOND
PHENOMENA.

74

HOW WILL YOU KNOW THE DIFFICULTIES OF BEING HUMAN,

IF YOU'RE ALWAYS
FLYING OFF TO BLUE PERFECTION?

WHERE
WILL YOU PLANT YOUR
GRIEF-SEEDS?
WE NEED

Ground

TO SCRAPE AND HOE, NOT THE SKY OF UNSPECIFIED DESIRE.

The wilderness way Moses took
was pure need and desolation.

*Remember how you cried*
*when you were a child?*

Joseph's path to the throne room of Egypt
where he distributed grain to his brothers
led through the pit his brothers left him in.

Don't look for new ways
to flee across the chessboard.
Listen to hear checkmate
spoken directly to you.

Mice nibble. That's what they need
to be doing. What do you need?
How will you impress the one
who gave you life?

If all you can do is crawl,
start crawling.

You have a hundred cynical fantasies
about God. Make them ninety-nine!

If you can't pray a real prayer, pray
hypocritically, full of doubt
and dry-mouthed.

GOD ACCEPTS
COUNTERFEIT
MONEY
AS THOUGH
IT WERE REAL!

This being human is a guest house. Every morning a new arrival.

A joy, a depression, a meanness, some momentary awareness comes as an unexpected visitor.

Welcome and attend them all! Even if they're a crowd of sorrows, who violently sweep your house empty of its furniture, still, treat each guest honorably. He may be clearing you out for some new delight.

The dark thought, the shame, the malice, meet them at the door laughing, and invite them in.

Be grateful for whoever comes, because each has been sent as a guide from beyond.

Welcome difficulty. Learn the alchemy True Human Beings know: the moment you accept what troubles you've been given, the door opens.

Welcome difficulty as a familiar comrade. Joke with torment brought by the Friend.

Sorrows are the rags of old clothes and jackets that serve to cover, and then are taken off. That undressing, and the beautiful naked body
          underneath,
               is the sweetness
                    that comes
                         after grief.

ne night a man was crying, Allah! Allah!
His lips grew sweet with the praising,
until a cynic said,
"So! I have heard you
calling out, but have you ever
gotten any response?"

The man had no answer to that.
He quit praying and fell into a confused sleep.

He dreamed he saw *Khidr,* the guide of souls,
in a thick green foliage.
                          "Why did you stop
praising?"
"Because I've never heard anything back."

                          "This longing
you express is the return message."

The grief you cry out from
draws you toward union.

Your pure sadness that wants help
is the secret cup.

Listen to the moan of a dog
for its master.
That whining is the connection.

There are love-dogs
no one knows the names of.

Give your life
to be one of them.

i

HONOR    THOSE

WHO    TRY

TO RID THEMSELVES    OF ANY LYING,

WHO EMPTY    THE SELF

AND HAVE ONLY    CLEAR BEING

THERE.

Forget your life.
　Say *God is Great*. Get up.
　You think you know
　what time it is.
　It's time to pray.
You've carved so many little figurines, too many.
Don't knock on any random door like a beggar.
Reach your long hand out
to another door, beyond where
you go on the street, the street
where everyone says, "How are you?"
and no one says How aren't you?

Tomorrow you'll see what you've broken and torn tonight,
thrashing in the dark. Inside you

there's an artist
you don't know about.
He's not interested in how things
look different in moonlight.

If you are here unfaithfully with us,
you're causing terrible damage.
If you've opened your loving to God's love,
you're helping people you don't know
and have never seen.

Is what I say true?
Say yes quickly,
if you know, if you've known it
from before the beginning of the universe.

These
spiritual windowshoppers,
    who idly ask, How much is that?
Oh, I'm just looking.

They handle  a hundred items
and put them down,
shadows with no capital.

What is spent is love
and two eyes wet
with weeping. But these walk
into a shop, and their whole lives
pass suddenly in that moment,
in that shop.

Where did you go? "Nowhere."
What did you have to eat? "Nothing
much."

Even if you don't know
what you want, buy something,
to be part
of the general exchange.

Start a huge, foolish, project,
like Noah.

It makes absolutely no
difference what people
think of you.

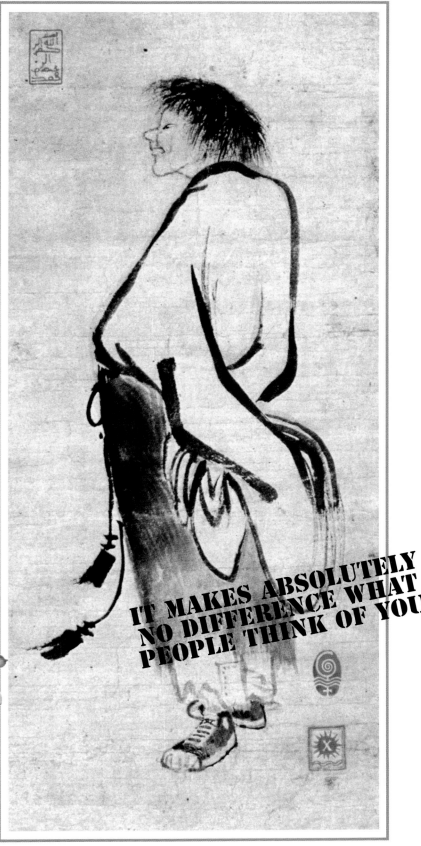

IT MAKES ABSOLUTELY
NO DIFFERENCE WHAT
PEOPLE THINK OF YOU

# I HAVE SUCH A TEACHER

74

## THE DIRECT WAY

The presence of the teacher puts you back in connection to God. Michael Green and I had the great good fortune to sit with Bawa Muhaiyaddeen, the Sufi master who came to Philadelphia in the 1970s, who first entered history as a jungle ascetic in Sri Lanka in the 1940s. His story begins when two pilgrims in the Katerengama Forest in southern Sri Lanka came upon a man sitting in a tree, whom they perceived immediately to be a light-being. They invited him to their village in the north. A month later, he walked into their dusty farm hamlet and began the public teaching that continued until his death on December 8, 1986. Bawa may have spent as many as fifty years in the jungle studying the ways of God as they appear in nature, in the plants and animals. Very little is known of his life before he was discovered by the two pilgrims. Nothing in the way of a conventional lineage or biography. He was a renewer of the way of direct connection. It is Bawa in the garden opposite, and on pages 88 and 117.

I would not have much understanding of, or feeling for, Rumi's poetry if I had not visited Bawa in Philadelphia sev-

eral times a year for several years. When we sat with him in his room, we felt the night ocean fill with glints of light. We were the place between the fish and the moon. He would sometimes end a discourse by saying, "God gives the truth. The mistakes are mine." We ask to be forgiven for the mistakes we've made here. Bawa Muhaiyaddeen felt that this was the time for Rumi to be brought to the West. We hope that this collaboration by two devotees is in the spirit of that insight, and we hope for the grace that will let us get out of the way and allow the inner qualities of our teacher, and Rumi and Shams, to come through.

By "teacher" Rumi can sometimes be pointing to the daily course of one's life: a room of calm people talking, the wind and thunder of rain on the way, ordinary moments, weather, dreams that guide our opening. He also might refer to an ecstatic ruby-mine moment when the lover feels the ocean's myriad dance inside.

The poem on the next page is Rumi's deathbed poem, a type of poem that is very common, almost a requirement for Zen masters, but rare in the Sufi tradition.

There's no way out,
no cure but death.
Last night in a dream
I saw an old man

standing in a garden.
It was all love.
He held out his hand and said,
Come toward me.

If there is a dragon on
this path,
that old man has
the emerald face

that can deflect it.

This is enough,
I am leaving my self.

83

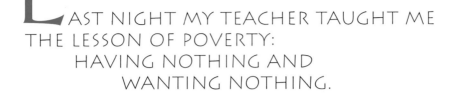

LAST NIGHT MY TEACHER TAUGHT ME
THE LESSON OF POVERTY:
    HAVING NOTHING AND
        WANTING NOTHING.

I AM A NAKED MAN STANDING
    INSIDE A MINE OF RUBIES,
        CLOTHED IN RED SILK.

I ABSORB THE SHINING
    AND NOW I SEE THE OCEAN,
        BILLIONS OF SIMULTANEOUS MOTIONS
        MOVING IN ME.

        A CIRCLE OF LOVELY QUIET PEOPLE
            BECOMES THE RING
                ON MY FINGER.

        THEN THE WIND AND THUNDER
            OF RAIN ON THE WAY.


                I HAVE SUCH A TEACHER.

Jasmine comes up where you step.
You breathe on dirt, and it sails off
like a kite. You wash your hands,
and the water you throw out
shines with gold.

You say a line of scripture,
and all the dead commentators
lift their heads.

Your robe brushes a thornbush,
and a deep chord of music comes.

Whatever you break finds itself
more intelligent for being broken.
Every second a new being
stands in the courtyard of your chest
like Adam, without father or mother,
but the beginning of many generations
to come.

I should rhyme that fifty times!

The beginning without any
inclination to end!

But I won't. I close my mouth
in hopes you'll open yours.

i was dead, then alive.
Weeping, then laughing.

The power of love came into me,
and I became fierce like a lion,
then tender like the evening star.

He said, "You're not mad enough.
You don't belong in this house."

I went wild and had to be tied up.
He said, "Still not wild enough
to stay with us."

I broke through another layer
into joyfulness.

He said, "It's not enough."
I died.

He said, "You're a clever little man,
full of fantasy and doubting."

I plucked out my feathers
and became a fool.

He said, "Now you're the candle
for this assembly."

But I'm no candle. Look!
I'm scattered smoke.

He said, "You are the sheikh,
the guide."
But I'm not a teacher. I have no power.

He said, "You already have wings.
I cannot give you wings."

But I wanted *his* wings.
I felt like some flightless chicken.

Then new events said to me,
"Don't move. A sublime generosity
is coming toward you."

And old love said, "Stay with me."
I said, "I will."

You are the fountain of the sun's light.
I am a willow shadow on the ground.
You make my raggedness silky.

One master drew this on the wall of his meditation cave, the winding road being the conventional path to union. The thinner shortcut line on the right is how it goes with the grace and help of a teacher. Notice the emptiness they both arrive at, and the sun!

IF THE LUMINOSITY OF THE SHEIKH'S FAITH
WERE TO ACTUALLY RISE IN THE EAST,

EVERYTHING BELOW THE CRUST OF THE EARTH
WOULD BECOME HANDFULS OF MYSTERY,

and everything above, a green lightedness.
Resplendent spirit,
or a body made from the ground,
which are you?

Tell me! I'm puzzled.
All this light, yet a body!

Who is the teacher?

Imagine the time the particle you are
returns where it came from!

The family darling comes home. Wine,
without being contained in cups, is handed around.

A red glint appears in a granite outcrop,
and suddenly the whole cliff turns to ruby.

At dawn I walked with a monk
on his way to the monastery.

"We do the same work," I told him.
"We suffer the same."

He gave me a bowl.
And I saw:

# THE SOUL HAS THIS SHAPE

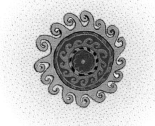

Shams
and actual sunlight,
help me now,
being in the middle of being partly in my self,
and partly outside.

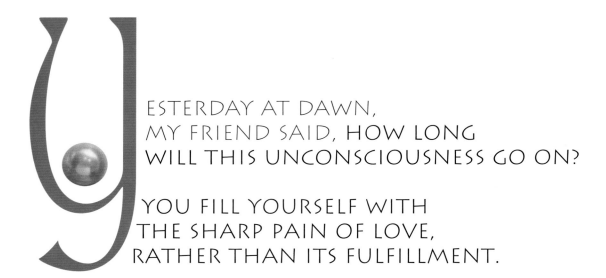ESTERDAY AT DAWN,
MY FRIEND SAID, HOW LONG
WILL THIS UNCONSCIOUSNESS GO ON?

YOU FILL YOURSELF WITH
THE SHARP PAIN OF LOVE,
RATHER THAN ITS FULFILLMENT.

I SAID, "BUT I CAN'T GET TO YOU!
YOU ARE THE WHOLE DARK NIGHT,
AND I AM A SINGLE CANDLE.

MY LIFE IS UPSIDE DOWN
BECAUSE OF YOU!"

THE FRIEND REPLIED, I AM
YOUR DEEPEST BEING.
QUIT TALKING ABOUT WANTING ME!

I SAID, "THEN WHAT IS THIS
RESTLESSNESS?"

THE FRIEND:

 DOES A DROP

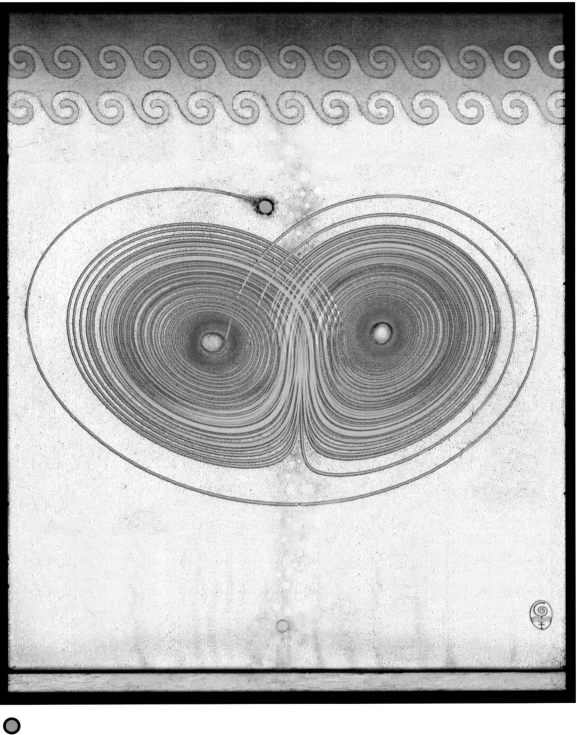

STAY STILL IN THE OCEAN?

MOVE WITH THE ENTIRETY,
AND WITH THE TINIEST PARTICULAR.

BE THE MOISTURE IN AN OYSTER
THAT HELPS TO FORM ONE PEARL.

Learn about your inner self from those who know such things,
but don't repeat verbatim what they say.
Zuleikha let everything be the name of Joseph, from celery seed
to aloeswood. She loved him so much she concealed his name
in many different phrases, the inner meanings
known only to her. When she said, The wax is softening
near the fire, she meant, My love is wanting me.

Or if she said, Look, the moon is up, or The willow has new leaves,
or The branches are trembling, or The coriander seeds
have caught fire, or The roses are opening,
or The king is in a good mood today, or Isn't that lucky?
Or The furniture needs dusting, or
The water-carrier is here, or It's almost daylight, or
These vegetables are perfect, or The bread needs more salt,
or The clouds seem to be moving against the wind,
or My head hurts, or My headache's better,
anything she praises, it's Joseph's touch she means,
any complaint, it's his being away.

When she's hungry, it's for him. Thirsty, his name is a sherbet.
Cold, he's a fur. This is what the Friend can do
when one is in such love. Sensual people use the holy names
often, but they don't work for them.
The miracle Jesus did by being the name of God,
Zuleikha felt in the name of Joseph.

When one is united to the core of another, to speak of that
is to breathe the name *hu*, empty of self and filled
    with love. As the saying goes, The pot drips what is in it.
        The saffron spice of connecting, laughter.
        The onion smell of separation, crying.
        Others have many things and people they love.
        This is not the way of Friend and friend.

92

# WE HAVE OPENED YOU

## AS THE SUN COMES UP

There are many window-like images in this book. These next poems celebrate the mystery of those openings. As meltdown occurs, a space is created that the true human beings visit, at ease, a caravanserai for the soul. And the art that grows from such Friendship is freeing, like David's melting down the chains. (David was known not only as psalmist and prophet, but as a metalworker.)

Rumi often describes this condition as Spring, and the sweetness of feeling outside of time. The cypress tree growing its slow, gigantic, cellular, circular life. Rumi recalls this Spring-day sense to remind us of the vast, balsamic weather we not only share, *we are*. The heart-openings become a living atmosphere and a haven for friends.

All of Rumi's poems can be seen, in one way or another, as nourishment for that inner gathering of friends. In this section, the *This–this* poem on page 106 was spoken at the end of a vigil, sitting in silence and *sohbet*, doing *zikr* and poetry.

As the sun came up, Rumi announced that this awareness was a majesty, or splendor, though he could only say what it was *not*: not joy or grief, not imagination, not euphoria, not a judgment place. The consciousness behind the poetry in this section comes from a realm of pure being that is prior to the existence of the universe and the source of it!

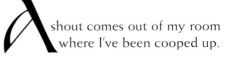

Friend, there's a window
    that opens from heart to heart,
        and there are ways of closing it

completely, not a needle's eye
    of access. Open or shut, both ways
        are sometimes appropriate.

The deepest ignorance is not to *know*
    *about* this window. When houses live
        side by side with windows open,

that's the embrace we want, a place where great souls
    can stopover and rest. I'll say just
        one more image and not explain.

*When David works with metal, he likes to melt down*
    *locks and chains and forge them*
        *into new shapes with his art.*

A shout comes out of my room
    where I've been cooped up.

After all my lust and dead living
I can still live with you.
You want me to.
You fix and bring me food.
You forget the way I've been.

The ocean moves and surges
in the heat of the middle of the day,
in the middle of the thought
I'm having.
Why aren't all human resistances
burning up with this thought?

It's a drum and arms waving.
It's a bonfire on the top edge of a hill,
this meeting again with you.

S pring, and everything outside is growing,
even the tall cypress tree.
We must not leave this place.
Around the lip of the cup we share, these words:

*My Life Is Not Mine*

If someone were to play music, it would
have to be very sweet.
We're drinking wine, but not through the lips.
We're sleeping it off, but not in bed.
Rub the cup across your forehead.
This day is outside living and dying.

Give up wanting what other people have.
That way you're safe.
"Where, where can I be safe?" you ask.

This is not a day for asking questions,
not a day on any calendar.
This day is conscious of itself.
This day is a lover, bread and gentleness,
more manifest than saying can say.

Thoughts take form with words,
but this daylight is beyond and before
thinking and imagining. Those two,
they are so thirsty, but this gives smoothness
to water. Their mouths are dry, and they are tired.

The rest of this poem is too blurry
for them to read.

**i** DO NOT KNOW WHO
LIVES HERE IN MY CHEST.

OR WHY THE SMILE COMES.

AM NOT MYSELF, MORE THE BARE
GREEN KNOB OF A ROSE THAT
LOST EVERY LEAF AND PETAL TO
THE MORNING WIND.

# Out Beyond Ideas of Wrong-doing & Right-doing

Out beyond ideas of
wrong-doing  &  right-doing
there is a field

I'll meet you there

When the soul lies down in that
grass
the world is too full to talk about.

Ideas, language, even the phrase,
each other

doesn't make any sense.

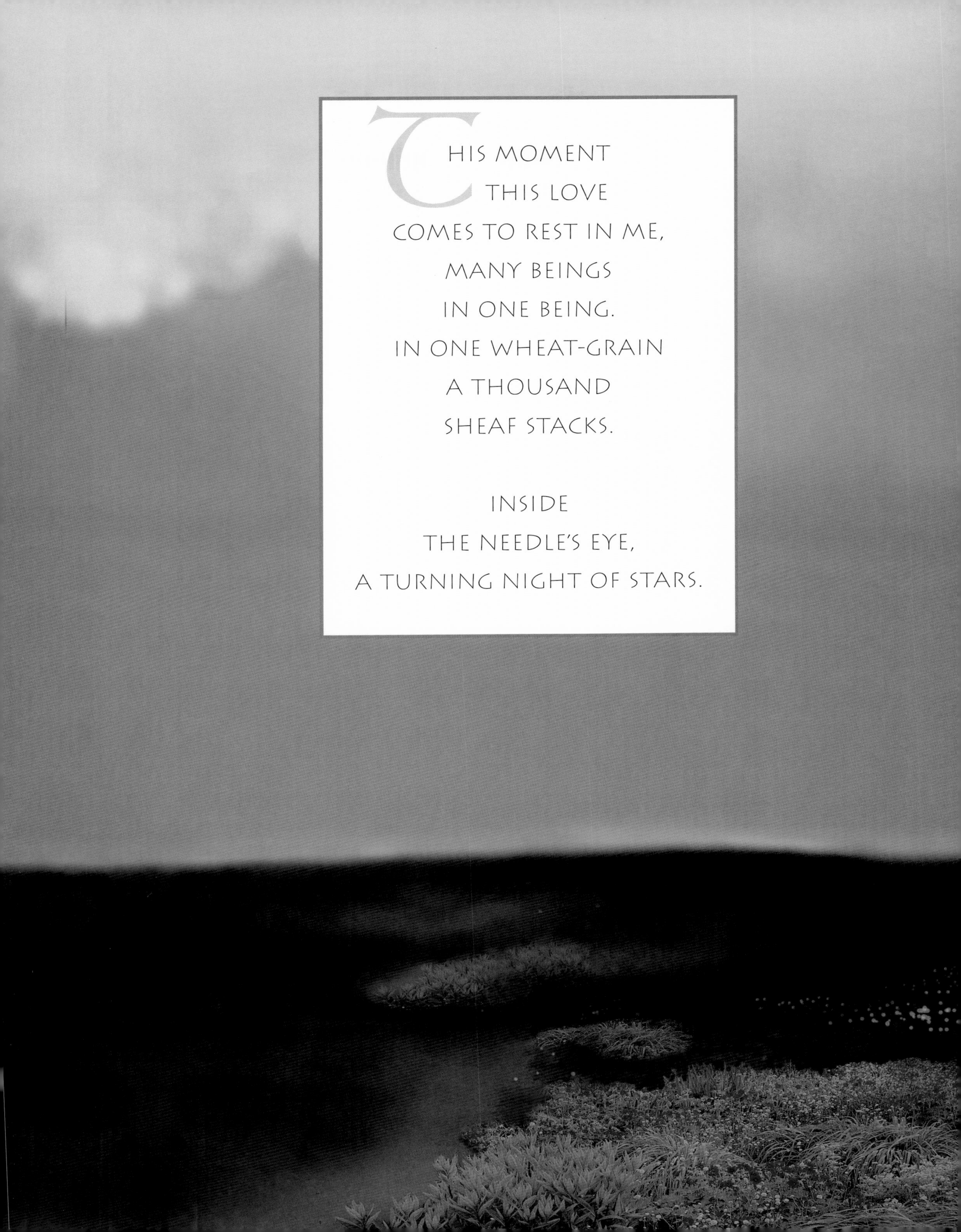

THIS MOMENT
THIS LOVE
COMES TO REST IN ME,
MANY BEINGS
IN ONE BEING.
IN ONE WHEAT-GRAIN
A THOUSAND
SHEAF STACKS.

INSIDE
THE NEEDLE'S EYE,
A TURNING NIGHT OF STARS.

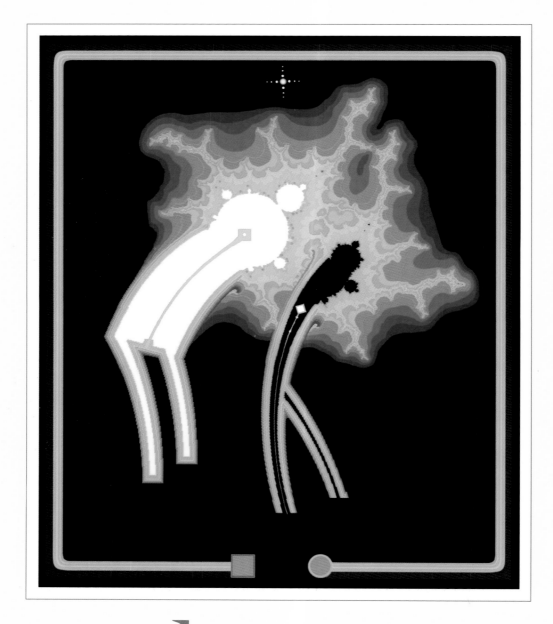

Lightning, your presence
from ground to sky.
No one knows what becomes of me,
when you take me so quickly.

Rumi and Shams are playing chess. Rumi realizes that in a couple of moves, he is going to be checkmated. "Oh, I've lost," he says in mock-despair. Shams suddenly looks at him, "You've won," and their Friendship goes to a deeper level of realization.

THE CLEAR BEAD AT THE CENTER
CHANGES EVERYTHING.
THERE ARE NO EDGES
TO MY LOVING NOW.

YOU'VE HEARD IT SAID THERE'S A WINDOW THAT OPENS
FROM ONE MIND TO ANOTHER,

BUT IF THERE'S NO WALL, THERE'S NO NEED
FOR FITTING THE WINDOW, OR THE LATCH

BEING

IS NOT WHAT IT SEEMS,

# NOR NON-BEING.

THE WORLD'S
EXISTENCE IS NOT
IN THE WORLD.

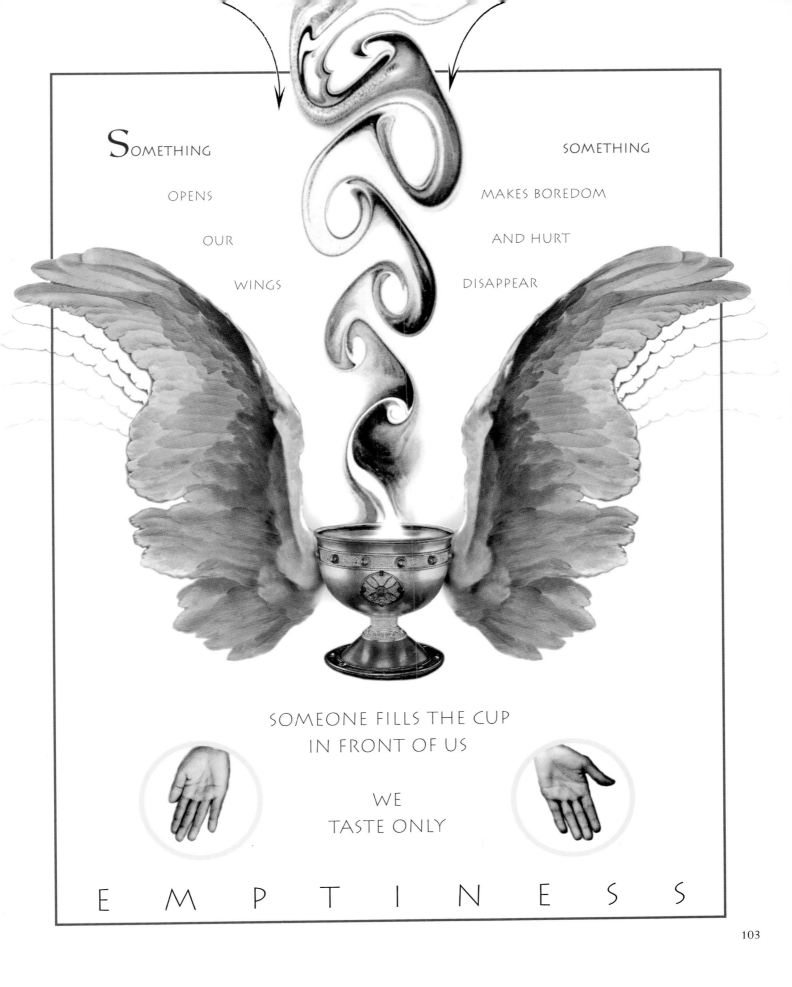

SOMETHING

OPENS

OUR

WINGS

SOMETHING

MAKES BOREDOM

AND HURT

DISAPPEAR

SOMEONE FILLS THE CUP
IN FRONT OF US

WE
TASTE ONLY

E   M   P   T   I   N   E   S   S

ESSENCE
IS EMPTINESS

EVERYTHING ELSE,
ACCIDENTAL.

EMPTINESS BRINGS PEACE
TO LOVING.
EVERYTHING ELSE, DISEASE.

IN THIS WORLD OF TRICKERY

EMPTINESS

IS WHAT YOUR SOUL WANTS.

# This

we have now
is not imagination.

## This

is not
grief or joy.

Not a judging state,
or an elation,
or sadness.

Those come
and go.

# This

is the presence that doesn't.

It's dawn, my friend,
here in the splendor of coral,
inside the Friend, in the simple truth
of what Hallaj said.

What else could human beings want?

When grapes turn to wine,
they're wanting

## This.

When the nightsky pours by,
it's really a crowd of beggars,
and they all want some of This!

# This

that we are now
created the body, cell by cell, like bees building a honeycomb.

The human body and the universe
grew from This, not

# This

from the universe and the human body.

For sixty years I have been forgetful every moment, but not for a second has this flowing toward me stopped or slowed. I deserve nothing. Today I recognize that I am the guest the mystics talk about. I play this living music for my Host. Everything today is for the Host.

# I am

dust particles in sunlight.
I am the round sun.

To the bits of dust I say, *Stay.*
To the sun, *Keep moving.*

I am morning mist,
and the breathing of evening.

I am wind in the top of a grove,
and surf on the cliff.

Mast, rudder, helmsman, and keel,
I am also the coral reef they founder on.

I am a tree with a trained parrot in its branches.
Silence, thought, and voice.

The musical air coming through a flute,
a spark off a stone, a flickering in metal.

Both candle and the moth
crazy around it.

Rose and the nightingale
lost in the fragrance.

I am all orders of being,
the circling galaxy,

the evolutionary intelligence,
the lift and the falling away.

What is and what isn't. You
who know Jelaluddin, you

the One in all, say
who I am.

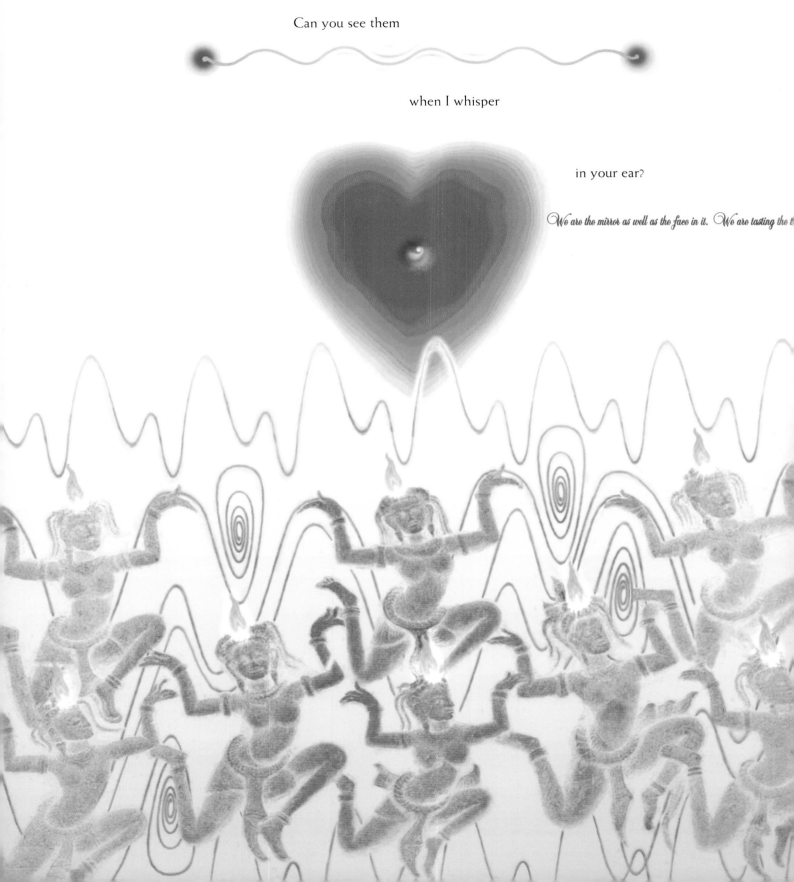

*O*aylight, full of small dancing particles
and the one great turning, our souls
are dancing with you, without feet, they dance.

Can you see them

when I whisper

in your ear?

*We are the mirror as well as the face in it. We are tasting the t* _nute of eternity . . . . . . . . . . the sweet cold water, and the jar that pours . . ._

WE ARE THE MIRROR
WE ARE TASTING THE TASTE
OF ETERNITY.
AND WHAT CURES PAIN.
AND THE JAR

AS WELL AS THE FACE IN IT.
THIS MINUTE
WE ARE PAIN
WE ARE THE SWEET COLD WATER
THAT POURS.

SOUL OF THE WORLD,
NO LIFE, NOR WORLD REMAIN,
NO BEAUTIFUL WOMEN AND MEN LONGING,

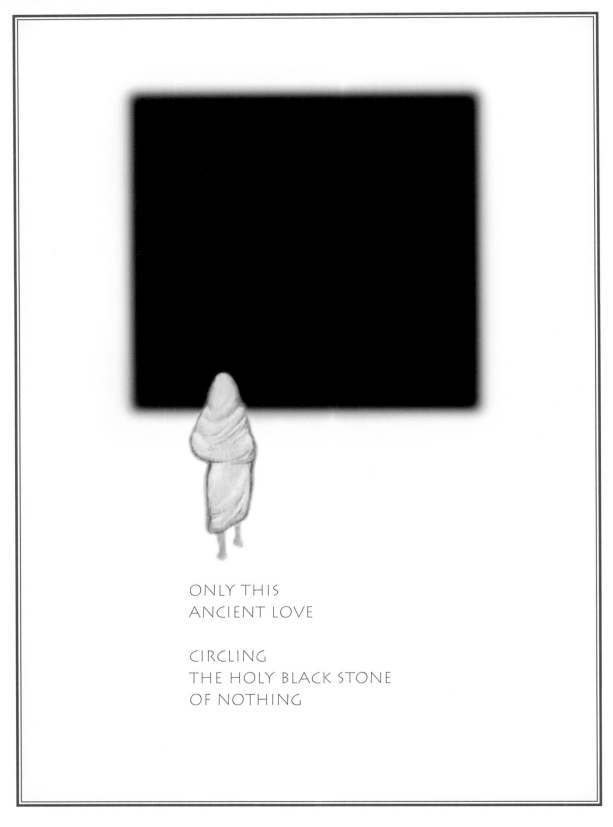

ONLY THIS
ANCIENT LOVE

CIRCLING
THE HOLY BLACK STONE
OF NOTHING

WHERE
THE LOVER
IS THE
LOVED,

THE HORIZON

AND EVERYTHING
WITHIN IT.

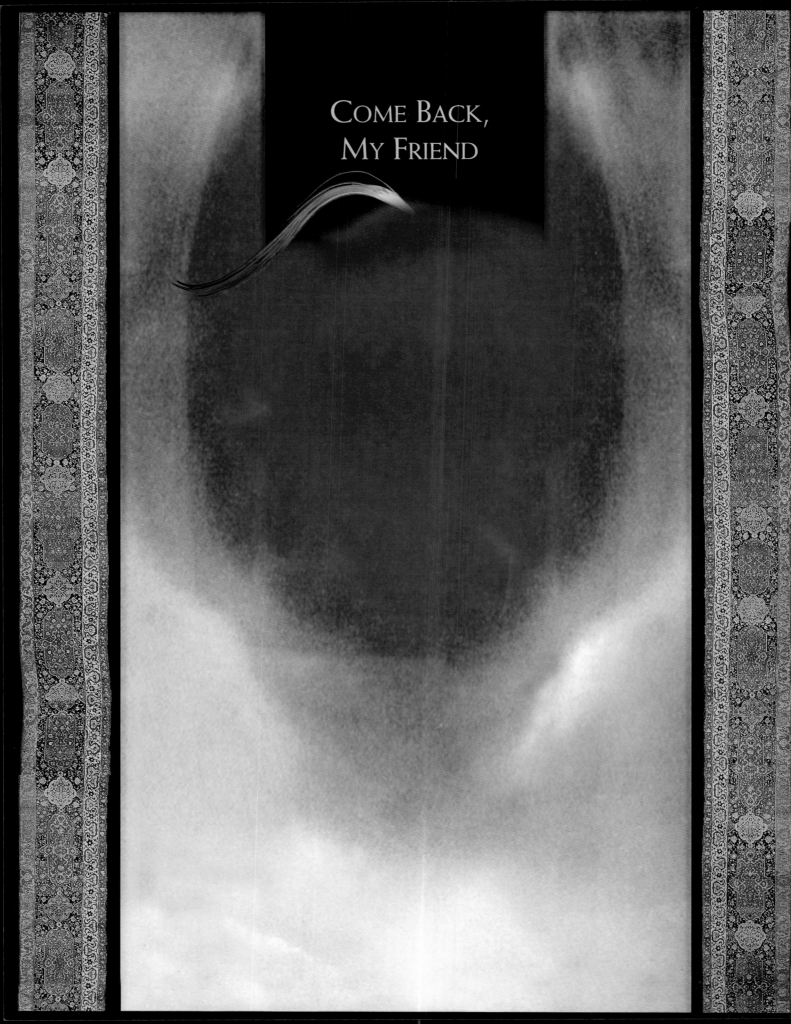

COME BACK,
MY FRIEND

From the hundreds of times I lost
the connection, I learn this:

your fragrance

brings me back. Inside that I become
a feast day with aloeswood burning,

the pure empty sky around the moon.

Then I make promises.

I break them.

And same as before,

I try

to find you
by thinking
and reading
about finding.

NO

HELP

THERE!

## TRY SOMETHING DIFFERENT

The story goes that Rumi, near the end of his life, was asked why, since he valued silence so much, he produced such a volume of language. He replied, "The radiant one inside me has never said a word." Call it a desert of vast solitude or a granary of communal grace, the source of Rumi's poems is what they give a taste of. One of his most frequent metaphors for it is an ocean without a shore, the medium that spawns and contains us. When we talk about God, we're like a school of fish discussing the possible existence of the sea! Rumi enjoys more the fluid freedom of swimming.

This is the point where you might set this book down and try something different. Try to discover what *fragrance* really is and what it might be to live inside *that*. Words and images can never give the experience. The *feel* of this Friendship gained from spiritual art may seem very familiar, a *virtual* reality, when it's not yet yours.

The dis-connection Rumi speaks of here, everyone understands. The re-connection with the *you* can only be lived.

What was in that candle's light
that opened and consumed me so quickly?

Come back, my friend. The form of our love
is not a created form.
Nothing can help me but that beauty.

There was a dawn I remember when my soul
heard something from your soul.

I drank water from your spring,
and felt the current take me.

FRIEND, OUR CLOSENESS IS THIS:

ANYWHERE YOU PUT YOUR FOOT

FEEL ME IN THE FIRMNESS UNDER YOU.

HOW IS IT

WITH THIS LOVE,

I SEE YOUR WORLD

AND NOT YOU?

Don't grieve.
Anything you lose comes round
in another form.
The child weaned from mother's milk
now drinks wine and honey mixed.

God's joy moves from unmarked box
to unmarked box, from cell to cell.
As rainwater, down into flowerbed.
As roses, up from ground.
Now it looks like a plate of rice and fish,
now a cliff covered with vines,
now a horse being saddled.
It hides within these, till one day
it cracks them open.

There's the light gold of wheat in the sun
and the gold of bread
made from that wheat.
I have neither. I'm only talking
about them,

as a town in the desert
looks up at stars on a clear night.

issolver of sugar,
    dissolve me,
      if this is the time.
        Do it gently with a touch
     of a hand, or a look.
Every morning I wait at dawn. That's
        when it's happened before.
Or do it suddenly like an execution.
How else can I get ready for death?

You breathe without a body like a spark.
You grieve, and I begin to feel lighter.
You keep me away with your arm,
but the keeping away is pulling me in.

YOU AND I HAVE SPOKEN ALL THESE WORDS,
BUT FOR THE WAY WE HAVE TO GO, WORDS ARE NO PREPARATION.

There's no getting ready,
other than grace.

My faults have stayed hidden:
One might call that a preparation!

I HAVE ONE
SMALL DROP
OF
KNOWING
IN MY
SOUL

LET IT
DISSOLVE
IN
YOUR
OCEAN.

There are so many threats to it.

Inside of us, there's a continual autumn. Our leaves fall
and are blown out over the water.
A crow sits in the blackened limbs
and talks about what's gone.

120

## THEN YOUR GENEROSITY
## RETURNS: SPRING, MOISTURE, INTELLIGENCE,
## THE SMELL OF HYACINTH AND CYPRESS

Joseph is back!

and then Jesus is breathing again.

And if you don't feel in yourself

Very little grows

the freshness of Joseph,

on jagged rock.

be Jacob!

Be ground.

Weep, and then smile.

Be crumbled,

Don't pretend

so wildflowers

to know something

will come up

you haven't experienced.

where you are.

There's a necessary dying,

Try something different.

S  U  R  R  E  N  D  E  R

Y ou've read where it says that
Lovers pray constantly.

Once a day, once a week, five times an hour,
is not enough. Fish like we are
need the ocean around us.

Do camel-bells say, Let's meet again
Thursday night?
Ridiculous. They jingle
together continuously,
talking while the camel walks.

Do you pay regular visits to yourself?
Don't argue or answer rationally.

Let us die,
and dying, reply.

INTO THE SOUP

FLAVOR

It has been said that what Shakespeare is to the English-speaking world, Rumi is for Persian speakers. Some poets embody a national soul: Rilke, Germany; Whitman, the United States; MacDiarmuid, Scotland; Yeats, Ireland; Neruda, Chile; but I would claim that Rumi belongs to a wider constituency, mystics of the world united! There is a grand generosity about the work. An improvisational wind blows through this poet that is weather beyond any cultural boundary.

He truly is "a naked man, standing inside a mine of rubies, clothed in red silk."

So what might be the purpose of this art? It's always unsatisfying to try to say, but maybe it's to celebrate a friendliness with soul, with spirit's being in a body, the mysterious Friendship of Rumi and Shams, the extravagant creativeness of life lived inside THAT, and the naturalness of it.

One Sufi teacher put the paradox this way: "God is the secret of human beings and human beings are the secret of God. Of all beings only humanity can realize God and God's wisdom. When that happens, God is man and man, God."

Rumi once likened the connection between the personal and the great self with that between chickpea and cook. If cooked long enough, and obviously that's the point, the chickpea becomes the cook, serving the table its transformed life.

A chickpea leaps almost
over the rim of the pot
where it's being boiled.

"Why are you doing this to me?"

The cook knocks him down with the ladle.

"Don't you try to jump out.
You think I'm torturing you.
I'm giving you flavor,
so you can mix with spices and rice
and be the lovely vitality of a human being.

Remember when you drank rain in the garden?
That was for this."

Grace first, sexual pleasure.
Then a boiling new life begins,
and the Friend has something good to eat.

Eventually the chickpea
will say to the cook,

                    "Boil me some more.
Hit me with the skimming spoon.
I can't do this by myself.

   I'm like an elephant that dreams of gardens
                    back in Hindustan
                    and doesn't pay attention
   to his driver. You're my cook, my driver,
                    my way into existence.

                    I love your cooking."

THE COOK SAYS,

      "I was once like you,
fresh from the ground. Then I
boiled in time,
and boiled in the body, two fierce
boilings.

My animal soul grew powerful.
I controlled it with practices,
and boiled some more, and boiled
once beyond that,

      and became your teacher."

S O, student and teacher keep blending and cooking, becoming sustenance for a deeper and wider awareness. Rumi adores this constantly transforming Friendship between the universe and the source moving through it. He addresses that elusiveness in the many appeals of the color red.

R ed with shyness, the red
that became all the rosegarden reds.

The red distance.
Red of the stove, and boiling water,

red of the mountain turning bloodred
now. Mountain holding rubies

secretly inside, should I love more
you or your modesty?

Red is how the mystery teases with revelation and friendship, with roses, mountain sunsets, the inside of a cooking stove, a galaxy, hidden rubies and absence. The first spring color is a tinge of red in the woods. Reds catch the eye and remain aloof. Roses do not satisfy the longing they enclose. Red is a sign of love's presence and simultaneously of how it's shy and stays apart.

I was once attracted to this way because it led me to see the beloved in everyone, and everywhere, glints of red. But Rumi says when that happens, *you* (the lover) become a barrier. Only when that distance dissolves and your ordinary life, with its longing, becomes the Friend—the longed for one—does the path unfold in a wider pattern.

A surprise birthday parade down Boulevard
for John Seawright's 40th in Athens, Georgia.

IF THE BELOVED IS EVERYWHERE,

THE LOVER IS A VEIL,

BUT WHEN LIVING ITSELF

BECOMES THE FRIEND,

LOVERS DISAPPEAR.

I HAVE NO MORE WORDS.

LET THE SOUL SPEAK
WITH THE SILENT ARTICULATION
OF A FACE.